The Idea of an Essay

Genres, Genders, and Giraffes

VOLUME TWO

ISBN: 978-7-030-00024-8
Cedarville University
Cedarville, Ohio 45314

Compiled By the Composition Committee:

Dan Clark
Melissa Faulkner
Heather Hill
Isaac Mayeux
Cyndi Messer
Julie Moore
Michelle Wood
Nellie Sullivan

Edited by:

Madison Grapes

Cover Created by:

Madison Grapes

TABLE OF CONTENTS

Dear Readers,

Welcome to Cedarville University. We are excited to have you in our composition classes. This anthology is meant to serve as a learning tool, and we will use it together over the course of this semester as we engage in the process of writing.

Cedarville University values writing. Regardless of your major, writing will be an intrinsic part of your education during your years at Cedarville, as it is a primary means of expressing clear, organized, critical thought. Perhaps more importantly, the writing you will do as part of your academic life will serve as practice for the various writing tasks each of you will complete as part of your chosen professions, as well as preparation for the writing you will do in your various communities, interpersonal relationships, and your daily devotions with God.

Cedarville University commits to preparing each of you to be successful writers by requiring a first-year composition course taught by a member of the English, Literature, and Modern Languages Department. As composition instructors, we recognize the excellent writing created in our classes, so we host an annual composition contest for students who completed the course during that year. The anthology you are about to read consists of the winners of that contest for the 2013-2014 academic year.

In the following pages, you will find models of university level writing, as well as examples of how to structure, organize, support, and document various genres of essays written for different purposes and with specific audiences in mind. We do not suggest these essays are perfect, as one of the most exciting aspects of writing is that it is a process that includes revision, so a text can always be improved upon or recreated as something different.

Each essay begins with an instructor's note that provides context for the essay and asks questions to prompt further ideas. The instructor's note is followed by a short biography of the student who wrote the essay to hopefully illustrate that, although these students are now published authors, they are not much different from you, the reader. You should find this encouraging. If these students can write successfully at the university level, then so can you.

Sincerely,

The Cedarville Composition Instructors

Cedarville University's Department of English, Literature, and Modern Languages

Hello from Cedarville University. Thank you for your interest in the Department of English, Literature, and Modern Languages. Our programs produce men and women who communicate effectively and think deeply, cross-culturally, and creatively about the ideas that have shaped and continue to shape our world.

Our mission is to challenge students to go beyond expectations. Henry David Thoreau once wrote that we hit only what we aim at and thus ought to aim at something high. We agree — aim high. Who will write the definitive scholarly treatment of Don DeLillo's work? Who will share Christ by teaching English to migrant workers in west Michigan? Where is this generation's C.S. Lewis or Flannery O'Connor? At Cedarville University, we want our students to aspire to such heights.

Meet Our Composition Instructors

Daniel Clark
Associate Professor of English

Biography

Professor Clark teaches courses in composition, advanced grammar, contemporary world literature, film, and the graphic novel. Along with Dr. Andrew Wiseman, Professor Clark developed Cedarville's foreign film series. He also serves as co-sponsor of Alpha Kappa Delta, Cedarville's chapter of Sigma Tau Delta, the International English Honor Society. Before coming to Cedarville, he taught at the University of Maryland Asian Division in Okinawa, Japan. He also taught English as a Second Language (ESL) at the Okinawa Prefectural Language Center. Professor Clark has been at Cedarville since 1999.

Education and Credentials

- M.A. in English, University of Tennessee at Chattanooga
- B.A. in Secondary Education (with proficiencies in English and Bible), Tennessee Temple University

Interests

- Theology
- Film and contemporary world literature
- Japanese culture
- Comics, comix, graphic novels, manga, and bandes dessinées
- The Atlanta Braves (chop on!)

Contact Information

- Email: clarkd@cedarville.edu

Melissa Faulkner
Associate Professor of English

Biography

Dr. Faulkner teaches Basic English, Composition, and Visual Rhetoric. She also serves as the coordinator for Writing Across the Curriculum. Her research interests include memoirs as retention and critical thinking tools, story analysis, and the organic connection between WAC programs and assessment. Dr. Faulkner has received multiple Excellence in Teaching awards, including one from the Southern Ohio Council of Higher Education.

Education and Credentials

- Ph.D., Miami University of Ohio
- M.A., Wright State University
- B.A., Wright State University

Contact Information

- Email: mfaulkner@cedarville.edu

Heather Hill
Assistant Professor of English

Biography

Dr. Hill taught at the University of Washington for four years before coming to Cedarville. Her research interests include composition theory and pedagogy, rhetorical genre studies, contemporary rhetorical theory, history of rhetoric, knowledge transfer, critical discourse analysis, language and identity, language ideology, the rhetoric of sports culture, qualitative research methods, student-athlete advocacy, indigenous language revitalization, and sociolinguistics.

Education and Credentials

- Ph.D. in English (rhetoric and composition),
  University of Washington
- M.A. in English (rhetoric and composition),
  University of Washington
- B.A. in English Literature, Western
  Washington University

Interests

- Riding horses

- Long distance running
- Seattle Mariners baseball
- UW Husky football and basketball

Contact Information
- Email: hhill@cedarville.edu

Isaac Mayeux
Assistant Professor of English

Biography

Isaac Mayeux has taught Composition at Cedarville since 2012. He also serves as the university's Director of Debate, Assistant Director of the Writing Center, and co-sponsor of Alpha Kappa Delta, Cedarville's chapter of Sigma Tau Delta, the International English Honor Society. Before coming to Cedarville, he taught Composition at the University of Dayton while studying for his M.A. He also taught English as a Second Language (ESL) in Seoul, South Korea for one year.

Education and Credentials

- M.A. in English and American Literature, University of Dayton

- B.A. in English, Cedarville University

Interests

- Graphic narrative (AKA comics)
- Animation
- Sport coats
- Christian poetics
- Complicated strategy board games
- Cultural criticism

Contact Information

- Email: isaacjmayeux@cedarville.edu

Cyndi Messer
Associate Professor of English

Biography

Professor Messer taught several years in secondary education before joining the faculty at Cedarville in 1998. She teaches general composition and literature courses as well as methods courses for future English teachers. She currently serves as the program coordinator for the Adolescent and Young Adult Language Arts (AYALA) majors and is a key contact for questions concerning the

English education program. She also serves as faculty advisor for *The Miracle*, Cedarville's yearbook.

Education and Credentials

- M.A. in English, Wright State University
- B.A. in English Education, Cedarville College

Interests

- Favorite Places Visited: Paris, Puerto Vallarta, and San Franciso
- Hobbies: playing board games with family, exercising, reading, playing piano, gathering family and friends around a bonfire
- Favorite Authors: C.S. Lewis, Amy Tan, Thomas Hardy, John Steinbeck, Marilynne Robinson, Erik Lawson, and Shakespeare

Contact Information

- Email: messerc@cedarville.edu

Julie Moore
Associate Professor of Literature

Biography

Professor Moore directs the University's Writing Center, and in 2008, she received the Dean's Service Award for her work. She is also the author of the poetry books, *Slipping Out of Bloom* and *Election Day*. Professor Moore has been nominated for the Best of the Net anthology and twice for the Pushcart Prize; she has also received the Editor's Choice Award from Writecorner Press, the Rosine Offen Memorial Award from the Free Lunch Arts Alliance, and the Janet B. McCabe Poetry Prize from Ruminate. You can learn more about her work at www.julielmoore.com.

Education and Credentials

- The Ohio Writing Project, Miami University
- M.A., University of Dayton
- B.A., Cedarville University

Interests

- Broadcasting poems on "Conrad's Corner" on WYSO, 91.3 FM

- Watching foreign films and movies based on literary works
- Cheering for the Philadelphia Phillies and Eagles

Contact Information

- Email: moorej@cedarville.edu

Nellie Sullivan
Assistant Professor of English

Biography

Helena "Nellie" Sullivan's poems, reviews, and translations have appeared in *eXchanges, Moist Towelette, Hover Project, Drunken Boat,* and *Shampoo.* At Cedarville, she teaches Poetry Workshop, Advanced Poetry Workshop, Contemporary Poetry, Introduction to Literature, and Freshman Composition. She has been at Cedarville since 2006.

Education and Credentials

- M.F.A. in Creative Writing with emphasis in poetry, University of Iowa
- B.S. in Cultural Anthropology and English Literature, Central Michigan University

Interests

- Travel/Road trips
- Canning food
- Film
- Lateral logic puzzles

- Illuminated manuscripts

Contact Information
- Email: helenasullivan@cedarville.edu

Michelle Wood
Associate Professor of English

Biography
Doctor Wood has been at Cedarville since 1995. Before coming to Cedarville, she taught English in Beijing, China. She has presented papers at national conferences, including the Conference on College Composition and Communication, the National Council of Teachers of English, the College English Association, and the Society for the Study of American Women Writers, speaking on topics such as Multigenre writing, Catharine Maria Sedgwick, Margaret Fuller, Alice Cary, and Amy Tan. Dr. Wood is a member of the Society for the Study of American Woman Writers and the Catharine Maria Sedgwick society.

Education and Credentials
- Ph.D. in Literature and Criticism, Indiana
  University of Pennsylvania

- M.A. in Composition and Rhetoric, Wright State University
- B.A. in English Education and Speech Education, Cedarville College

Interests

- Travel
- Biking
- Archival research of women's life-writing
- College football

Contact Information

- Email: woodm@cedarville.edu

Narratives/Memoirs

"My Teacher, Poetry" by Rebecca Kersjes

Instructor's Notes

In her literacy narrative, Rebecca Kersjes successfully uses detail, dialogue, and description to tell a story about her road to becoming a literate person. Her journey through time ends in the present day, helping to tease out the significance of her story. It can be often be difficult to convey critical thinking through story telling. If you were peer reviewing this essay, what advice might you give Rebecca to increase the evidence of critical thinking in her story?

Writer's Biography

Rebecca Kersjes is a third-year Language Arts Education major from Cincinnati, Ohio. Over the years, Rebecca developed a love for writing poems, but currently her favorite style of creative writing is nonfiction prose. In her free time, she enjoys spending time exploring the woods or baking with friends.

My Teacher, Poetry

It is possible to write an entire poem about the way a drop of rain lands on the ground or the beauty of dust dancing in the light streaming through a window. Poetry taught me to see the beauty in everything around me because when I notice these small, beautiful moments, I can write. And when I can find a way to put these moments perfectly into words, I can allow others to experience what I have experienced, and hopefully they will be able to find these beautiful moments in their own life.

When an English teacher said, "Writing is difficult, it takes time and it doesn't come easy," I didn't understand at first. I didn't understand because I hadn't taken the next step in writing - the step of moving forward from good, satisfactory writing to beautiful, purposeful writing. As poetry taught me to see the tiny details of life around me it also taught me that each word in a sentence or stanza matters. I had to test each line out loud before I was satisfied. The exact place the word lies on the page even matters. I realized that if I was to become the writer I dreamed to be I needed to learn to put careful thought into each word I wrote.

For years, I expressed my thoughts best through writing; whether in the form of a poem, or thoughts scribbled down illegibly as I tried to pour everything that was inside my head onto the paper in front of me. It was a release, a safe haven, a place I could let every thought go. These thoughts I wrote down became a secret place for my mind to escape. Yet, a part of myself wanted to let someone else in to see what I had revealed. I struggled to share any of this writing. I thought it was petty and insignificant. When I read through anything I had written it lacked what I thought good writing needed, but I could never seem to break out of the cycle of mundane, boring expressions. It seemed plain and obvious. Too obvious. What you saw is what you got, and that really didn't appeal to my senses the way I wanted.

Still, I continued to write. Good or bad, writing seemed to be a part of who I was through my beginning years of high school. As I look back, I see that writing was a journey I undertook. It was sometimes easy and progressive, I sailed smoothly through poems and stories like the way water slides over stones in a river. Other times writing was painstaking and slow. I had trouble writing anything at all, and if I could come up with anything, it didn't satisfy me. When I read what I forced myself to write it was bland and tasteless, lacking the creativity and fullness good writing requires. It wasn't until I started sharing my writing that I was able to appreciate the beauty behind it and realize my writing had worth and value to other people, not just myself.

Public speaking has never been easy for me. I remember perfectly the first time I shared a poem to a group of people. I showed my youth pastor at church a poem I had written because it matched up with the message he had just preached.

Joe looked at me excitedly "You have to share this with the teens upstairs next service."

I looked at him nervously, "No way, I can't do that."

But I couldn't help but smile. He thought it was good – good enough to share with the other teens. That meant it had some worth and value, something that I had never realized my poetry had. I seemed torn in two; I wasn't sure if I was ready to open myself up to a crowd of teenagers that could, and surely would, judge me. But the other half of me was excited to see what would happen when I let others see the way I saw the world through poetry. So I said yes.

I found myself standing in front of a room of teenagers mixed with several adults looking at me, expecting me to say something of worth to them. I could feel the heat of nervousness boiling over inside me as my palms began to sweat. I s-s-stuttered my way through each word, bouncing back and forth from one foot to the other. My eyes clung to the words like a lifeline to avoid the all too real stares of everyone in the room. It felt like I couldn't get any words out right. They seemed to either all jumble together too quickly, or stick in my throat, refusing to come out. But then it was over, as quickly as it had begun.

It was until later that I realized I had actually enjoyed sharing my poem in front of a group. I never would have thought that sharing something that I had kept private for so long could be freeing. Despite the satisfaction of that moment, though, I continued to struggle to share my writing in front of people. In class, in church, or even with close friends, it was difficult. What I have learned over the past few years is that even though it may be a struggle to open up my heart for everyone to see, whenever I do only good has come from it. It has helped me grow closer to those around me, helped me connect with new friends and new teachers. It has always been taught in school that we as students need to become better writers. But what I realized is that, though my writing style has improved greatly, writing was my teacher. Poetry taught me to see the world in a different light. I learned that in order to understand the big things in life, I must first notice the seemingly small, insignificant things that I would usually pass over.

Taking criticism from others was always a struggle for me because it took so much courage for me to even share it in the first place. Then when they would critique what I had showed them I seemed to put up the wall again. In time, I realized that not opening myself up to others criticism was holding me back from improving. Poetry again taught me something. Many times I refused to see the mistakes I made, and letting others in to point them out should be considered helpful, not hurtful. Allowing myself to acknowledge the mistakes I made gave me the opportunity to continually grow and change my style of writing. I was able to find the places that felt not only the most natural, but worked the most successfully.

Writing was a treasure I held onto dearly. It took me on a journey through the years that I never imagined possible. Putting words onto a page seems like such a simple concept, and maybe it is, but it taught me so much more than creating a well flowing sentence. Beauty appeared around me in the simplest of things or ideas as I realized that the most skillful writing comes from taking the time to notice this always-present beauty of life. Poetry taught me to appreciate the small moments in life so that when I formed these moments into a work of art on a page others could then see these moments in their own life. After years of struggling to write what I thought was poetry worth sharing, poetry now takes my hand and leads me step by step through each special moment in my life and stops me when I begin to rush, saying "Take the time to write this down, so when the moment is long gone and you're feeling lost, you can come back to this moment, and it will be as if it never left you."

"~~Double Triple~~ Many Lives" by Faithe Smiley

Instructor's Notes

Faithe Smiley tells her readers a story about story telling in her literacy narrative. Detail, dialogue, and description, or the 3Ds, are necessary to effectively draw readers into a story, set a scene, develop characters, and reveal universal significance. Point to examples in this essay where Faithe incorporated each of the 3Ds. Identify places where she might have included even more.

Writer's Biography

Faithe Smiley is a returning junior English major from Pittsburgh, Pennsylvania. Faithe mostly enjoys creative writing, but also appreciates the challenge of exploring many other styles and forms of writing. In her spare time, she likes writing and reading books. She spends her summers working at a summer day camp run by her church, but hopes to go on another missions trip during a summer in the near future.

~~Double Triple~~ Many Lives

I was in preschool when I heard my first stories. They came in the form of stories from the Bible read to us in Sunday School. They were short: only about a dozen sentences each. But because they were short it is now easy to identify each of the three elements of good writing within them. Each began with a main character who had a problem. After a little dialogue between characters, God would help them solve their problem, and the conflict was resolved. At the end of each story was a question meant to convey the significance of the story because preschoolers have to be prompted in order to consider such things. Questions like, "How does God help you in your life?"

I do not remember hearing these stories. I only know they were read to me because I work in Sunday School classes and hear them being read to the children I work with. What I do remember, my earliest memories, in fact, are those of my mom reading aloud to me, my sister, and my brother. When we were very young, she read us picture books: *Chrysanthemum, Fritz and the Beautiful Ponies, The Day Jimmy's Boa Ate the Wash, Stellaluna, Ferdinand the Bull, Julius the Baby of the World, The Velveteen Rabbit, The Giving Tree,* her favorite, *Love You Forever,* and my favorite, *Andrew Henry's Meadow.* We loved to listen to her; not only for the sake of being together, but also for the sake of the story itself.

My sister and I quickly advanced in our reading skills. We leapt past *Dick and Jane*, and quickly moved on to more difficult and much more entertaining stories. My brother, on the other hand, got stuck. He was bored out of his mind by *Dick and Jane* because the books of *Dick and Jane* are not stories. Each is a conglomerate of repetitive sentences designed to be a tool to teach young children basic reading skills without truly entertaining or engaging them in any way. My mom quickly realized that she was getting nowhere, so she revised his reading list and filled it with *Calvin and Hobbes* collections. His reading immediately improved. However, even though he could now read well, my brother still enjoyed having me read to him. We would sit side by side with a *Calvin and Hobbes* book across our laps and I would read it to him panel by panel. I used funny voices, sound effects, dramatic pauses, and changes in volume to make the words come to life.

Even though I could read on my own, I too still enjoyed being read to. As we got older, my mom began to read chapter books to us. I remember sitting on our back porch in the summer listening to her read *The Chronicles of Narnia*. I do not know if it was the first set of chapter books she decided to read to us, but I distinctly remember a moment when I was contemplating where to look. Before, I had curled up next to her and looked at the pictures from under her elbow. But now there were no pictures. I remember that it was then that I first began to stare dreamily out into the distance and see the pictures the words painted in my mind's eye.

This became a reflex for me, even when I began to read on my own. My imagination became so vivid, that sometimes I could barely see the words before me. I became a fly on the wall in Cair Paravel, Erebor, The Capitol, Lothlórien, Maycomb, Cawdor Castle, Ithaka, a raft on the Mississippi, West Egg, Manor Farm, Ingolstadt, behind the barricade in Paris, and many other captivating places. I saw what there was to be seen, I heard what was said, I smelled the flowers growing, I felt the wind on my face. When I was bored, I would daydream. My family would take long car trips and I would stare out the window: my eyes watched the world slide past but in my mind I was a world away.

In middle school I attended a small, private Christian school called Blackburn Study Center. We read many difficult books, including *The Epic of Gilgamesh, The Odyssey, The Canterbury Tales*, several writings of the Bard, and other classical works that are at times hard to understand. Although the people at Blackburn were all good students, not all of them were good at reading. Some would give up, others would fail to comprehend. My teacher had us discuss the assigned reading so that she could be certain that everyone was on the same page, both literally and figuratively. Eventually, it became inevitable that when these discussions began, everyone would look at me. It may be thanks to my habit of imagining each scene from every book I read, or some other reason, but I have great reading comprehension and retention. As it turned out, I would end up giving a quick summary of whatever it was we were supposed to have read the night before. I would insert my own commentary into the summary, making parallels to previous sections, giving a deeper explanation of the motives of certain characters, and all in all trying not only to explain, but also to entertain.

I kept in touch with the teacher of that class, mainly because she is my aunt. One day I was emailing her a paper I had written for one of my college classes so that she could give me some advice. She is an English teacher at Geneva College as well as Blackburn Study Center so she gives good advice about writing. After we had talked about the paper for a little while, I asked, "How are things going at Blackburn these days?"

"We have a bunch of new students this year," she replied. "I still teach Ancient Literature, but the class isn't the same without you. Not only would you discuss the readings, you would tell the story to the other students. With enthusiasm!"

I did not do so for the grade, I did it to bring those other students into the world I had imagined so that they too could see what there was to be seen and hear what was said and smell the flowers growing and feel the wind on their faces. I had begun to turn into a storyteller.

Finally, I began to write my own stories. These were the first writings I had ever done outside of school. As I wrote, of course, I tried to write well. Not just with good grammar or syntax, not simply 'well' in the sense of following the rules. I tried to write in a way that I thought people would want to read. Because I was a storyteller; I wanted to tell stories.

I knew the basic structure of a good story from the stories I had heard as a little preschooler in Sunday School class. I loved to read, and now to write, simply for the sake of a good story, because my mom had taught me to love stories all those years ago. I knew how to make my words come to life so that the reader would hear funny voices, sound effects, dramatic pauses, and changes in volume because of the time I had spent reading to my brother. Also through my mom reading to me, I had developed a rich imagination. As I wrote, I imagined every scene, every minute, and every move each character made. I played these scenes over and over again in my head, studying them, considering them, viewing them from every angle. I did not write a story until I had lived it.

That is what being a storyteller is all about. That is what being a reader is all about. When it comes to stories, reading and writing is about more than simply relaying information or even entertaining. It is about getting out of our own heads and living in a different world. Through stories, we can live the lives of a knight in shining armor, a princess in a tower, a slave on a cotton plantation, a misunderstood evil villain, a great explorer, and a skillful magician all in one day.

In *The Lion, the Witch, and the Wardrobe*, by C.S. Lewis, the main characters, the Pevensie children, travel through a magical wardrobe to another world. Specifically, they travel to a country called Narnia, which they save from an evil witch, and are subsequently crowned kings and queens of Narnia. They proceed to grow up until one day, they rediscover the wardrobe and emerge back into our world at the exact moment at which they left it, children once again. The book is full of allegorical language and general life lessons; but overall, it teaches that books allow us to live entire lives in other worlds without ever leaving ours.

And this is what I find so enchanting about reading and writing stories. In this life, they are the closest we will ever come to immortality.

"Diabetes: The Birth of a Reader"
by Meredith Oxley

Instructor's Notes

Personal narratives are generally told from the first person point of view, which is exactly what Meredith Oxley does in her literacy narrative. But what would happen if Meredith told her story from another character's point of view? What if she wrote from her mom's perspective? Would the story still be true? If one of the reasons we write is to learn, what learning might occur if Meredith rewrote this story from her mom's point of view? What if the story was written from the point of view of an inanimate object, perhaps from that of Meredith's insulin syringe? Is that even a possibility?

Writer's Biography

Meredith Oxley is a junior Nursing major from Ohio. After her undergraduate studies she hopes to pursue a career as a diabetes educator because of her personal experience with type 1 diabetes. She is also fascinated by the liberal arts and enjoys reading classics in her spare time. Her hobbies include cooking, playing sports with friends, reading, and spending time with her family.

Diabetes: The Birth of a Reader

On June 23, 2011, I went in for a checkup at the doctor's office. I had been experiencing some odd physical signs: excessive tiredness, constant dehydration, and unnatural weight loss. Nothing greatly worried me; nevertheless, my mother wanted to make sure everything was alright. Instead of going home after my appointment like I, a healthy teenager, had expected, I was rushed to the emergency room. That day I was diagnosed with type 1 diabetes.

During the second half of the previous school year, I had experienced a lot of emotional stress, positive and negative; mostly negative. My grandfather passed away two days before my sixteenth birthday in January, I took a two week long trip to Europe in March,

I had been dealing with the breakup of a friendship at church, and I had to manage my devilishly heavy schoolwork load. Apparently, in addition to all these events, I was obliviously experiencing symptoms of my diabetes the last few months of the school year. All that together within six months wore me out emotionally and physically.

On the day of my diagnosis, my mom and I sat in a little yellow room at my doctor's office, exotic animal photos ornamenting the walls and children's books filling the shelves beside our chairs. We waited for my pediatrician, Dr. Bockhorn, to come and hopefully give us an explanation for my unusual, unexplained symptoms. The tall, slender, smiling doctor came in and proceeded with her usual checkup procedure. As she was looking over my vital signs that the nurse had taken and examining my ears, nose, and throat, we chatted some. In our conversation, we touched on how emotionally depressed I had been that year with all the commotion and stress. By the end of our discussion, Dr. Bockhorn suggested that I seek counseling to help me become "stable" again. I firmly rejected this proposal in my mind and was overwhelmed by the thought of meeting with a counselor. I tried to deny this need, but all I could do was cry again as I had done so many times that year. Resorting to tears had become second nature to me in the past six months. After this conversation concluded, she gave me a cup and sent me off to the bathroom. I came back with the specimen to be tested. My mom and I were once again left alone in the room. It was quiet except for the almost whispered dialogue between the two of us. With tears in my eyes and a stuffy nose, I said, "Mom, I don't want to do anything this summer." It wasn't long until Dr. Bockhorn returned. She came in, looked me in the eye, and directly said, "I've found glucose in your urine, and I suggest that you go to the emergency room immediately." I had no idea what this meant at the time because I was so flustered. I turned to Mom, and silently asked, "What?" She responded with a shocked expression on her face, but still calmly said, "It means you might have diabetes."

I cried the whole ride to the hospital. My eyes burned at this point. Looking out the window, I could see the sun shining in the bright blue sky and people walking down the streets. It was a lovely day, and I had originally planned to enjoy it like a normal teenager would have. I even considered getting a group of friends together to go to the neighborhood pool and play some pickup basketball at the park nearby. Instead, I was on my way to the emergency room because my blood sugar was over 700 milliliters per deciliter. In the car I told Mom again, this time with sobs in between words, "I don't want to do anything this summer. No camps, no activities. Nothing." She looked at me and reassuringly said that it was okay. I was free to do absolutely nothing.

We arrived at the hospital, and I received the first of my many insulin injections. I don't remember much about those first three or four hours in the emergency room. All I do recall is lying on this extremely flat bed with few covers. My mom sat on my left in a chair, speaking to me softly as I cried the hardest I have ever cried. Many different nurses and doctors came to me during that time, informing us on the latest updates and blood sugar levels. During those long hours in the ER, my pastor came to visit. This big, tall man, wearing his Texas Longhorn shirt, sat down and prayed over me.

Finally, I was admitted to the hospital, and we all got settled into our room. The situation was not an ideal one. I had to spend the night in this crammed hospital room wearing that awful thin gown with people coming in periodically to prick my finger and stab me with a needle. To add to my pleasures, I was put in the only room on that floor that had double occupancy. A dark blue curtain divided the two sides of the room. Even though my family did not interact with the other family and we did not see each other, it was just another annoyance to the whole event. Not only did the poor group on the other side have to put up with my family, but my family and I had to listen to their choices in TV shows. At one point we could overhear the loud shouting of people on that obnoxious *Maury* show. It was a nightmare. It felt to me like everything was spinning and spinning, and all I wanted was stillness and quiet.

During my time at the hospital, many friends came to visit me. It was heartening to see how many people cared and wanted to encourage me during this troubling time. A number of them even brought me gifts or items of theirs to entertain me. Kevin and Victoria, my youth pastor and his wife, also came to visit. They brought a great variety of things to keep me occupied while sitting in this overcrowded, plain little hospital room for hours on end. Victoria specifically brought me her own collection of Jane Austen's novels. This item will always stand out in my memory because it sparked a wonderful and powerful new passion within me that summer.

I never had the time to read any of the books while at the hospital because thankfully I was released after one day. In that one day, I was bombarded with a multitude of information about this new diagnosis of type 1 diabetes. Then I was sent home having to put all this information into practice immediately. I had to learn and live a completely new lifestyle. Despite this overwhelming experience, I knew my summer was now free for me to do anything I wanted. I did not sign up for any camps; I was not going to do summer reading homework. I was going to simply sit down on my couch at home and read this borrowed book: *Pride and Prejudice.*

It was about the time when my family and I returned home from the hospital that my eyesight started deteriorating. For about two weeks or more, my whole vision was fuzzy. The doctors said it probably resulted from my dramatic blood sugar change. My glucose levels were so high for so long that my body had adjusted to the new level. Now that the levels were back down to normal, my body had to readapt which caused this strange blurriness of vision. I could still see people, but it was like I was wearing glasses with horribly unclear lenses. Basically, I couldn't read anything. So, my plan to read for relaxation did not work out as I had intended. However, I was firmly determined to get through this book. I ended up buying a set of Jane Austen's novels on CD. Every time my mom and I were in the car together, we would listen to the CD, hearing the different characters being played out through different voices. I was finally able to "read" like I wanted.

After about two weeks, my eyesight came back to me— clear once again. I began to actually read the pages of this Jane Austen book, soaking in the words of the story. By the end of the book, I was in love. I realized how enjoyable reading could be. Back in elementary school, I read a lot, but I lost this passion for reading by my middle school years. Up until my diagnosis, I had not really thought much about reading for fun. But, there was something about all the craziness that was going on that called me back to it. All I had wanted to do for weeks now was read. And so that is what I did. Next, I picked up *Sense and Sensibility*. It wasn't long until I finished that one and picked up another one. This progression went on all summer long. My daily position consisted of me sitting on my soft, light brown couch in the reclined position, a red fleece blanket covering my legs, the dogs barking in the backyard, and the sun shining in through the window. By the end of that summer, I had read all six of Austen's novels, and I still craved more.

Looking back on that summer, I remember all those raw emotions from my diagnosis: stress, shock, fear, anger, confusion. By far, it was the hardest event that I have experienced, but it has also been one of the most beneficial. Because of my diabetes, I have acquired many new passions, and I have been molded into the person I am today. I appreciate the work of authors far more than I would have without that stressful year in 2011. Because of these books I read, I finally received the rest I needed. Because of the literature, I dealt with my life changes in a peaceful manner. Even though that summer was a transition time, learning to manage my blood sugar every moment of each day, I had my fictional companions and their worlds in which they lived. I could simply drift away into these imaginary realms when needed, and I did.

Because of that doctor's appointment, I discovered my diabetes. Because of my diabetes, I discovered my beloved books. For me, the classic Jane Austen became my companion and comforter that hectic summer. Since my encounter with her, I've come to know and love many others, finding pleasure in their works, seeking their company when I am feeling down. Reflecting back on that summer, I am thankful for that trial of being diagnosed, because without it, I may never have come to love and appreciate books as I do now.

"Getting There" by Aubrey Gillette

Instructor's Notes

This essay is an example of a Literacy Memoir. The instructor asked Aubrey and her classmates to write an essay that explored how a literacy event made a lasting impact on the writer's life. Often times a school assignment becomes more meaningful than we could ever have imagined. How does Aubrey's high school composition assignment allow her to discover important ideas about herself, her goals in life, and her future? How do the two "desk" scenes that Aubrey represents in the essay demonstrate her maturing process to readers? Why might this personal essay have value for a reader?

Writer's Biography

Aubrey is a sophomore Psychology major from Grand Rapids, Michigan. She loves learning, especially through reading, and she collects lessons from the mentors in her life. Aubrey enjoys both long distance mission trips and local adventures in the great outdoors. Her highest priorities in life include her relationships with her Creator and with her loved ones.

Getting There

Hundreds of little feet ran down the dry, orange dirt road, eager to get to the clinic. The muggy air did not prevent the children from hustling across the rocks and mud into town.

"Muzungu! Muzungu!" the mass of children yelled, referring to the white people they spotted through the crowd.

The muzungus, Americans, constructed a small clinic to remove jiggers—nasty flea-like critters—by jabbing a metal surgical utensil through layers of skin and tearing out the bugs from their little feet before providing them with shoes to wear home. Wherever their home was. Some of these feet walked home to small huts. Others were not so fortunate. Many of the children would return to the orphanage up the road, after they received their brand new pair of shoes. Regardless of their direction, those small, sore feet would take baby steps the whole way.

Over 7,000 miles away, in an air-conditioned home, I sat in a swivel desk chair with my feet grazing the carpet as I kicked them back and forth under the computer desk. Amidst my endless contemplation of millions of little feet around the world searching for a home, I found myself taking baby steps of my own. I read about the jigger clinics in Uganda in my free time because of my interest in third-world missions and medical relief. Little did I know that my interest in missions would connect to the research paper I was writing about international adoption. In my composition class, I was assigned to research a topic that had major societal implications. After researching, I was required to write a persuasive essay explaining why my reader should or should not choose, in the case of my topic, international adoption.

Hours a day sitting at the wood desk in my home office, staring at the blurry white computer screen and looking for just the right article to suit my topic left me bewildered, lost even. I felt immobilized by the statistics before my eyes; the situation was worse than I thought. Researching international adoption turned out to be a life-altering experience for me at the age of seventeen, just one year older than the cut-off for adoption.

In the afternoons between school and work, I felt exhausted during the hours of staring at the computer screen. I selected research articles, found applicable quotations, and worked towards figuring out how to put them into a logical sequence that would articulate the point I was trying to make: that Americans should make international adoption a priority.

On one particular afternoon, I sat in my home office with *Bonanza, Gunsmoke*, or some other old western television show playing on the T.V. to the left. My dad relaxed in the leather chair behind me at his glass top desk, snacking on cheese and crackers, eyes glued to the T.V. screen in the corner. I felt an overload of distraction in the room, but I had to focus so that I could type. I struggled to coax my overwhelming feelings out through my fingers and onto the computer keyboard. I wanted to express the ache I felt for the shoeless, homeless, motherless, and fatherless children of this world. I clicked my black Paper Mate pen continuously while

I thought, scribbling out bad ideas and jotting down thoughts that would help me convey a feeling that words could hardly describe. It was a messy process, characterized by many long afternoons staring at a pile of papers and hoping for the ability to make sense of the statistics and case studies. While I dug through piles of research, children around the world were digging through piles of trash that must have reeked of animal carcasses. They were searching for any small piece of edible substance they could find. Those children were wandering the streets as I wandered the Internet, both of us searching, but for different resources.

"Dad, can you turn the T.V. down? My brain hurts," I murmured.

Before putting another cracker in his mouth, the old man grumbled, "Yeah, sure. How long are you going to need the computer? I have to check my email."

My dad: always preoccupied and rarely concerned. In that moment I wished I could tell him how much importance this project had in my heart, but he would never understand. He sat comfortably in our home, surrounded by a fair amount of money and few medical concerns. I doubted if he ever cared about the sick, poor, and needy people that lived half a world away. I also feared his imminent discouragement of the route I wanted to take in life, the route towards counseling and providing physical and emotional care for the needy. He would never be the muzungu that showed up in an African village to remove jiggers from the feet of crying children, and he would never want me to be that muzungu either.

I determined in that moment to reject my father's negative opinion. I invested my emotions into my research project. From that point on, I would take baby steps toward the mission field. One night, a few weeks after the day in the home office with my dad, I was sitting cross-legged on my cozy twin bed, studying articles about orphans. During my reading, I resolved to adopt one or two African babies someday. My dad would not like it, but that would not restrict me.

Maybe, I thought to myself, *by making African babies his grandchildren, I could somehow influence his opinion in the future.*

The statistics, the stories, and the faces of little motherless children made my skin itch with discomfort, causing me to squirm atop my bed.

I cannot tolerate this. I cannot accept the reality that so any children are living without parents while Americans, myself included, sit in contentment.

Baby steps, I decided. Baby steps would take me to those children and lead me to the opportunity of loving them with more than just knowledge of them. I would love them with my hugs and my words, and I would use whatever abilities I could to change their lives, even if that meant adopting them as my own.

After a couple of months of investing my time and energy into researching international adoption, I still found myself working for hours at the desk in my home office. The more interested I had become in the topic, the more I longed to act. I was finally writing the persuasive essay, which meant sitting in the desk chair with my face nearly pressed against the screen as I typed carefully, eager to include the most precise words that would support my argument. This was not just any old research project my blonde, middle-aged, intimidatingly strict Advanced Placement Language and Composition teacher assigned. Not anymore. Rather, it grew into an opportunity for me to gain an understanding of the lifestyle I chose to pursue. My desire grew from wanting to make the needs of the poor and fatherless known to wanting to spend much of my future meeting those exact needs. My focus was no longer about the topic of international adoption. It was so much more. Adoption, missions, human trafficking, medical relief, and world hunger filled my thoughts during those final days of essay revision and nit picking.

Upon completion of this five-month research assignment, I began taking baby steps toward my future career. I committed to studying cross-cultural Psychology at Cedarville University to develop more awareness of people from other cultures and backgrounds. I also aspired to involve myself in ministry, no matter my age or location. This aspiration would lead to the opportunity for mission involvement. I would take baby steps: first be active in a church and other ministries through college, next keep my ears open for the chance to take part in a trip or project, then go.

As a result of taking these ministry baby steps, I have had epiphanies and discoveries while sitting at my desk. However, I have moved on to a desk of my own. I no longer sit at the desk in my parents' house with my dad observing my research. Now, my desk is my safe place. I make my own decisions while sitting there in my small, white-wall dorm room.

I made one big decision on a brisk Thursday morning near the end of January. I sat with a cup of black coffee in my hand, reading my Bible, which lay open on my desk. Upon finishing my reading, I closed my eyes to pray.

Lord, keep me on the narrow path, I prayed, referring to Matthew 7:14.

Suddenly it dawned on me.

The narrow path leads to Uganda.

In that moment, I committed to traveling to Uganda during the summer of 2014, just another step on my way to a life of cross-cultural ministry. My research project during the second semester of my senior year of high school stimulated more than knowledge of international adoption. My life plans developed during that time. I realized that I want to be more than a Psychologist who works in America with middle and upper class Caucasians discussing their battles with depression and marriage tensions. I learned I could do so much more, including global missions, counseling human trafficking victims, or even partnering with a non-profit organization to do counseling in jigger relief clinics.

Although my upcoming mission trip is not through Sole Hope, the organization providing jigger relief and shoes to children in Uganda, I hope to experience a similar atmosphere to that of their clinic scenes. I long to hear the children shouting with excitement, to play soccer and dance and sing with them. I found my life goal through my research on international adoption.

I want to be the reason children shout "Muzungu!"

Analysis/Response Essays

"Integration Paper"
by Breanne Brigadoi

Instructor's Notes

In this paper, Breanne uses Rhetorical Genre Theory to analyze and critique the field of nursing in an effort to discover the ways that she may need to actively resist the ideologies and assumptions held within those disciplines. Drawing on texts both in genre theory and on topics surrounding Christians in academic fields, she answers questions such questions as: What does it mean to say that genres portray community ideology? How might you resist genre conventions that portray ideologies that you disagree with? What are the specific disciplinary ideologies that you may need to actively resist? What might be some of the consequences of that resistance? How might you positively integrate your faith into the work of your discipline? What might be the reaction to that integration? Etc. The paper is organized into two sections: the first section talks in general about the ideas of genre and ideology, and genre critique and resistance, and then the paper moves on to talking about the nursing discipline and the specifics of the ideologies that she may need to resist and how she might positively integrate her beliefs into the nursing field. This organizational structure is probably much more complex than things you wrote in high school. If you were going to outline this paper, what might the outline look like? Why was this an effective organizational structure for this paper?

Writer's Biography

Breanne Brigadoi is a first-year Nursing major and a cadet in the Air Force ROTC program. Breanne has learned to enjoy academic writing and hopes to improve her writing skills as her college career continues. Her hobbies include working out, playing soccer, watching Disney movies, spending time with friends and family, and scrapbooking.

Integration Paper

Recently scholars of the composition community have become interested in the concepts of ideology and resistance that take place in various professional communities. There is much discussion over how communities use their genres to portray their ideology and how genre critique uncovers these belief systems. Furthermore, the idea of resistance to these ideologies has become a hot topic of debate, especially when it comes to Christians participating in secular communities. More research is needed in order to show how members of a community analyze their discipline in order to discover its ideology and then choose to resist these ideologies in a way that integrates their own belief system into their discipline. This is especially true for Christians, who often times find themselves participating in secular disciplines whose ideology, to some extent, disagrees with their faith. Therefore, this paper will be discussing the function of genre and how members, especially Christians, can effectively participate in a community whose ideology can be resisted, specifically in the professional field of Nursing. This will be accomplished by first discussing genre ideology, resistance, and analysis and then applying these thoughts to Christians in the discipline of Nursing. This will be done in order to prove that members of a professional community need to know the ideology of their discipline, how to resist those ideologies, the consequences of that resistance, and how they can be successful in integrating their faith into their profession.

The main purpose of genre is to express unity in a discourse community by portraying the ideology of the group. Bawarshi states that genres are, "ideological configurations that are realized in their articulation, as they are used by writers (and readers)" (9). In this case, ideology is the shared goals and beliefs of the community, a community made up of readers and writers. Bawarshi describes discourse community as, "the social and rhetorical environment within which cognitive habits, goals, assumptions, and values are shared by participants who employ common discourse strategies for communicating and practicing these cognitive habits, goals, assumptions, and values" (5). In other words, discourse communities are unified through common ways of communicating, and these modes of communication allow the ideology to be expressed and shared throughout the group. These communities can be social, political, recreational, professional, or academic; also, we can be born into some communities while others we voluntarily join. Despite the differences between these various communities, the concept of genre demonstrating ideology acts as the unifying factor. Ann Johns, for example, expresses the significance of genre within a discourse community. She says, "These communities use written discourses that enable members to keep in touch with each other, carry on discussions, explore controversies, and advance their aims; the genres are their vehicles for communication" (503). As we can see from this quote, genre acts as the primary mode for members to communicate effectively with one another and share their goals. As a result, the genres that are used by the community focuses on uniting the group in communicating language, practices, values, conventions, and principles that they all share. In other words, genre is used to express ideology of the group.

Genres act as a mean to unify a community by portraying ideology, but they also can be resisted and changed within the community. The dynamic quality of genres and their ability to be resisted has been discussed by several writing scholars. For example, Bawarshi defines genre as not just merely a classification system for sorting different types of writing, but "instead that genres are dynamic discursive formations in which ideology is naturalized and realized in specific social actions, relations, and subjectivities" (8). This means that genre is always changing and its purpose is to address ideologies specific to certain situations and audiences. These situations and audiences change over time, but they also can be changed through resistance shown by the members of the community. Ann Johns discusses the power of this resistance. She says, "communities and their genres are useful to study….because they are evolving: through affiliation of new, different members; through changes in authority; through anticonventionalism, dialogue and critique" (516). This means that within these communities, genre is constantly being resisted and adapting to the members' diversity, shifting ideologies, explored controversies, and changing authorities of the group. So as a result, the conventional use of the genre can be resisted, or fought against, because of various oppositions displayed by members of the group. This concept of resistance becomes increasingly important for Christians in a secular community,

42

because often times they find themselves in opposition with specific ideologies that are realized by the group's use of genre. This leads into the next point about genre, in that they should be analyzed and critiqued by members of the group.

Genres that are used by a community should always be analyzed and critiqued by members of the group so that members are aware of the underlying belief system that the genre wishes to convey and naturalize. It is through this critiquing that members decide if they wish to support or resist the group's ideology. Bawarshi discusses the importance of genre analysis; he says, "I offer genre analysis as a way for students to access, position themselves within, and participate critically in genred discursive spaces and the commitments, relations, identities, and activities embedded within them" (14). In this quote, Bawarshi is emphasizing the importance of genre analysis because that is the way that members fully realize their identity within the group and decide how they will contribute and participate as a member. For Christians in a secular world, it's important for them to undertake genre analysis in order to discover the underlying belief system of the academic or professional community they are involved in. Even if the secular community claims to possess ideology that is detached from religion, Edlin argues that, "The philosophical and presuppositional foundations of every subject emanate from a set of religious convictions that need to be exposed and critiqued" (207). This quote argues that every discipline operates under a belief system involving some kind of religious conviction. As a result, we can imply from this quote that through genre analysis, Christians can recognize the religious convictions their secular community actively or passively displays and ultimately decide if they agree or disagree and choose to resist those convictions. Overall, members of a community should always critique their discipline in order to uncover its ideology and decide for themselves how they will respond to it.

After taking a closer look at how genre portrays ideology and how ideology can be resisted, one can conclude that it's important for members of a community to undergo genre analysis in order to expose these ideologies and ultimately decide where they stand in relation to those beliefs. After having established this background of genre, the rest of this paper will now analyze and critique the professional discipline of Nursing, focusing on its ideology. This critique will be done in order to discuss how Christians might resist certain ideologies portrayed by genres in the Nursing profession, the consequences of the resistance, and how Christians can make a positive contribution to the field while integrating their faith into their profession.

For a Christian in the Nursing profession, the ideology of the discipline in many ways lines up with the beliefs found in the Christian faith and is portrayed through the use of multiple genres found in the field of Nursing. The ideology of the Nursing profession can be summarized in its Code of Ethics, which is established by the ANA (American Nurses Association). A code of ethics is, "A set of guiding principles that all members of a profession accept. It is a collective statement about the group's expectations and standards of behavior" (Potter and Perry 287). According to the ANA, the ideology of the Nursing profession is defined by the following terms: beneficence, nonmaleficence, justice, fidelity, autonomy, advocacy, responsibility, accountability, and confidentiality (286-288). Beneficence is defined as keeping the best interests of the patient more important than self-interests, in other words, doing good to others. Nonmaleficence is the avoidance of harm or hurt, or treating others as you would want to be treated; this is portrayed through the use of Nurse Practice Acts, which are professional nursing guidelines issued by the state. Justice is another term for fairness, such as staying unbiased and treating everyone with equality; nurses show this through their embrace of federal and state legislation regarding health care, such as the Americans with Disabilities Act (ADA). Fidelity refers to keeping promises and following through with plans; this is shown through use of organized Care Plans designed by the nurse that are individual to each patient. Autonomy refers to the patient's independence, or the right to decide as an individual; this is demonstrated by the use of consent forms that a patient agrees or refuses to sign regarding treatment or medical procedures. Confidentiality includes privacy rights and honesty in conduct; this is portrayed by the use of HIPAA legislation, which gives patients greater access to and control over their medical records. Lastly, advocacy, responsibility, and accountability refer to the professional behavior that all nurses should portray. All of these components of the Nursing ideology share common features with Christian teachings, such as integrity in conduct, doing good to others, treating others as you would want to be treated, equality under God, and freedom of choice. Although most, if not all, of the Nursing ideology is compatible with Christians, one of these components in particular, autonomy, usually becomes a problem that causes Christians to resist in the discipline.

Many Christians in the profession of Nursing find themselves resisting the ideology component of autonomy because of the ethical dilemmas that often are associated with it. Autonomy includes the right of the patient to decide about his or her medical care. This is indeed a very important right of every citizen, but it often tends to lead to medical questions of morality. Regarding controversial issues such as homosexuality, physician-assisted suicide, and especially abortion, medical personnel often find themselves asking questions of "Should we do this?" rather than "Can we do this?" (Orr 49). In other words, the morality of the caregiver comes into conflict with the patient's right of autonomy. This is especially a problem for Christians in the medical field because Christians possess moral beliefs that are not subjective, contrary to the world's view of individualized morality. Mark Cherry explains this by saying, "Contemporary biomedical ethics places persons, rather than God, in authority to define the right, the good, and the virtuous…cardinal moral value is instead assigned to individual liberty conceptualized as autonomous self-determination" (27). In this quote we can see that the right of autonomy refers to the patient's medical decision based on his or her liberty of individual morals. In this context, patients often demand medical treatments, such as abortion, even if the caregiver is morally against it, claiming that their right of autonomy would be violated if the treatment was refused. This poses a problem for medical professionals because autonomy refers to the patient's right to refuse a treatment (through not signing a consent form), not demand specific treatment. These ethical dilemmas based on the patient's right of autonomy cause many Christians to resist in the discipline of Nursing. Fortunately, many Christians can successfully resist under the defense of the Right of Conscience. Robert Orr states that, "The right of conscience is the right of an individual to refuse to do something requested by another based on his or her own conscience or religious beliefs….The medical right of conscience has been codified in U.S. medicine, U.S. federal law, U.S. state laws, international law, and international medicine"

(Orr 50-51). Based on this, Christians can refuse to participate or assist in medical procedures, such as abortion, because it violates their right of conscience. There are, however, many exceptions and legal issues regarding this right, and there is also much debate over the elimination of this right. And unfortunately, there are also consequences that come to Christians when they resist by using the right of conscience.

When Christians in the medical field resist the ideology of autonomy, they often suffer harsh criticism by the secular world, resulting in some negative consequences. They are labeled as intolerant to the moral standards of others and unprofessional in the medical setting. Sharon Crowley argues, "The conservative Christian response to difference is too intolerant. Christian conservatives wish to impose a standard of moral behavior on all of us so that they can easily discern- and disciple- those who depart from it" (104). This quote frames Christians as strict moral policeman whose only goal is to point fingers at sinners and accuse them of their wrongdoings. In the medical field, the same situation happens as well, described by Tristram Engelhardt, saying, "The condemnation by traditional Christian health care professionals of some lifestyle choices and narratives as immoral is regarded by the secular culture as unacceptably intolerant" (97). We can see from these quotes that the consequence of resisting moral autonomy in a secular world results in being labeled as intolerant. This is a problem for Christians because postmodern tolerance demands respect in all aspects, so tolerance to the world can be summed up by saying, "There is no definite right or wrong, so let's respect each other because we're both right in our own way". On the other hand, Christian tolerance has a very different perspective, in that it believes in an overarching, non-subjective truth of right and wrong– the truth that comes from the Bible. As a result, Christians in the medical profession are often labeled as intolerant, and as a result, they are considered unprofessional. The good news is that even though Christians may suffer these consequences, there is still hope that they can successfully integrate their faith into their profession and get positive reactions from others rather than negative ones.

Christian nurses can easily integrate their faith into the profession of Nursing by several means. One way is to actively demonstrate the ideology of Nursing that lines up with the Christian faith and doctrine, such as beneficence, nonmaleficence, justice, fidelity, advocacy, responsibility, and accountability. This will not only exemplify the qualities of a good nurse, but also the qualities of a genuine Christian. There are also opportunities for Christians to share their faith in the profession of Nursing. According to *The Fundamentals of Nursing,* a nurse doesn't just provide care and support for a patient's physical needs; they also are called to care for a patient's mental and spiritual needs as well (Potter and Perry 1-3). This means that if a patient wants to pray with a nurse or talk about spiritual things, the nurse is more than welcome to pray and share their testimony as a way to meet the spiritual needs of the patient, if the situation calls for it. Even though opportunities like this can be rare, a Christian nurse should always display the love of Christ in all they do in order to serve as a witness for the Christian faith. Lizabeth Rand says, "Witnesses are called to testify that without the unconditional love and forgiveness offered to them through Christ, they would be nothing" (359). Indeed Christian nurses should also follow this example by keeping a humble and compassionate attitude when working in their discipline. By doing this, others will notice the difference they display and will hopefully have a positive reaction towards the Christian nurse's faith. Opportunities like these allow nurses to integrate their faith into the discipline of Nursing.

After taking a closer look at genre, ideology, and resistance, one can conclude that genre analysis and critique is crucial for members to be successful in their profession. By genre analysis, the ideology of the group is enacted and uncovered for members, especially Christians, to agree or disagree with and ultimately decide if that ideology should be resisted. It's then up to the member to find a way to resist the ideology while integrating their faith into their profession. This will continue to be a topic of debate as more research is done to show how Christian nurses accomplish this in their profession.

Works Cited

Bawarshi, Anis S. "Introduction: A Meditation on Beginnings." *Genre and the Invention of the Writer*. Logan: Utah State UP, 2003. 1-15. Print.

Cherry, Mark J. "Sex, Abortion, And Infanticide: The Gulf Between The Secular And The Divine." *Christian Bioethics: Non-Ecumenical Studies In Medical Morality* 17.1 (2011): 25-46. Religion and Philosophy Collection. Web. 21 Oct. 2013.

Crowley, Sharon. "Tolerance And The Christian Right." *Communication & Critical/Cultural Studies* 4.1 (2007): 102-105. Print.

Edlin, Richard J. "Keeping The Faith: The Christian Scholar In The Academy In A Postmodern World." *Christian Higher Education* 8.3 (2009): 203-224. Print.

Engelhardt, Tristram H. "Christian Bioethics In A Post-Christian World: Facing The Challenges." *Christian Bioethics: Non-Ecumenical Studies In Medical Morality* 18.1 (2012): 93-114. Academic Search Complete. Web. 21 Oct. 2013.

Johns, Ann M. "Discourse Communities and Communities of Practice: Membership, Conflict, and Diversity", *Writing about Writing: A College Reader.* Wardle, Elizabeth, and Doug Downs Eds. Boston: Bedford/St. Martin's, 2011. 498-518. Print.

Orr, Robert D. "Medical Ethics And The Faith Factor: The Endangered Right Of Conscience." *Ethics & Medicine: An International Journal Of Bioethics* 26.1 (2010): 49-54. Academic Search Complete. Web. 21 Oct. 2013

Potter, Perry, Stockert, and Amy Hall. *Fundamentals of Nursing.* St. Louis: Mosby, 2013. Print.

Rand, Lizabeth A. "Enacting Faith: Evangelical Discourse And The Discipline Of Composition Studies." *College Composition And Communication* 52.3 (2001): 349-367. Print.

"The Desolation of *The Hobbit*"
by William Keating

Instructor's Notes

For this essay, William Keating needed to write an example of textual analysis. William chose to analyze a classic novel. What do you think about the assertions he makes about Tolkien's classical text? Does he provide sufficient support for his assertions? How does he structure his essay so he can both analyze and evaluate as opposed to just summarizing and describing?

Writer's Biography

William Keating is a chemistry major from Missouri who plans to graduate in 2016. He enjoys playing basketball and watching the Cardinals play baseball. William also loves reading Tolkien's works set in Middle Earth.

The Desolation of *The Hobbit*

"If An Unexpected Journey was a galumphing orc, smashing its way through the plot, The Desolation of Smaug is a fleet-footed elf, leaping through the trees," says Chris Barsanti in his article "The Hobbit: The Desolation of Smaug" (par. 8). In his article he suggests that Peter Jackson's *The Hobbit: The Desolation of Smaug* is an improvement from the first movie of Jackson's trilogy of movies being produced to depict J.R.R. Tolkien's famous novel, *The Hobbit*. Barsanti suggests the improvement is due to the liberties Jackson took that left out much of Tolkien's descriptive scenes and to the many new characters that Jackson brings from the book and from his own embellishment of The Hobbit (pars. 3-6). Barsanti is not the only one who commends Jackson's second hobbit movie; many are claiming *The Hobbit: The Desolation of Smaug* outshines its predecessor. Todd McCarthy's article "The Hobbit: The Desolation of Smaug" agrees with Barsanti and the majority of reviewers that Jackson's second movie was exceptional because of its addition of characters, and he adds that the fast pace increases the movie's quality (pars. 2-5). While all these voices praise *The Hobbit: The Desolation of Smaug*, I disagree and insist that the movie was disappointing.

As I sat through the showing of T*he Hobbit: The Desolation of Smaug*, I could almost hear the s*nip, snip, snip* of Peter Jackson's scissors as he cut apart Tolkien's masterful work. The first reason Jackson's production disappointed viewers was its poor rendering of the book it supposedly portrayed. He made his first mistake by changing the plot. Sometimes producers may find it necessary to adapt a plot when they illustrate a book as movie, but Jackson made changes in terrible places. He removed several of the most exciting and character-developing scenes in the story. For example in Tolkien's novel, the main character, Bilbo, is alone when his companions are caught by spiders, and he must combat the spiders and rescue his friends. This is a key moment in Bilbo's character development because throughout the book he learns to become independent and courageous, but Jackson condensed Bilbo's role in defeating the spiders through cunning tactics and replaced it with unimportant characters driving away the spiders and saving the dwarves. Jackson cut meaning from *The Hobbit*. Another major plot change Jackson introduced to his version of *The Hobbit* included the group of dwarves with whom Bilbo is traveling entering their old mountain home which is inhabited by a dragon named Smaug. Apparently Jackson did not think logically when he shredded *The Hobbit* because the point of Bilbo going on the journey with the dwarves was to be the burglar to sneak into the dragon's lair and steal back the coveted treasure of the dwarves. In the Tolkien's novel Bilbo is the only one who can slip past the dragon because he discovers a ring that makes him invisible, and even then he barely escapes Smaug's lair alive. Jackson clipped out logic from *The Hobbit*. These were just a few of the changes made to the original tale which made the plot illogical and shallow.

Peter Jackson not only drastically changed the plot, he also added bland characters. Owen Gleiberman in the article "The Hobbit: The Desolation of Smaug" published in *Entertainment Weekly* explains that Jackson risked the quality of the movie by adding his own character, Tauriel, but also declares that by infusing romance into the story the risk yielded reward (par. 3). I agree that Jackson's move was a risk, but I do not think that his decision improved the movie or can be justified. Adding characters might not always be detrimental to a movie, but the characters Jackson added deadened the movie. Tales inspire readers and viewers when the author or producer introduces fresh ideas, but Jackson's added characters accomplished the opposite. An elf named Tauriel was added as a love-interest for one of the dwarves, Kili, in the journeying company, but all the other dwarves and elves are very disdainful of the other respective group. Tauriel and Kili are "star-crossed lovers," and their relationship is stale and predictable. Jackson also gives the elf, Legolas, who is not mentioned in *The Hobbit,* a cameo appearance. Legolas was a prominent character in *The Lord of the Rings* and is related in Tolkien's books to one of the characters who is in *The Hobbit.* A short appearance would have been fine, but Jackson alters the plotline again to simply incorporate a character from one of his older movies. Jackson could have spent the screen time on important scenes from *The Hobbit* rather than making time just to add an unoriginal character and point to his previous trilogy. Jackson crops out portions of *The Hobbit* to make room for an overused character.

The second reason I argue others overrated *The Hobbit: the Desolation of Smaug* is that it incorporated ridiculous impossibilities to add thrill. Perhaps if Jackson had left Tolkien's original piece more intact, he would not have needed to add his own impractical action scenes to fill the gaps he created. While the setting of the movie is a mythical place, Middle Earth, it does not justify the mindless action Jackson threw into the plot. At first the movie did not have too many implausible happenings, but as the movie progressed, the impossible action sequences multiplied. Midway through the story the dwarves escape the dungeons of the elves in barrels floating down a river, but they are pursued by orcs and their previous captors. A battle ensues between the three groups. The scene includes an elf balancing on one leg on a dwarf's head sticking out of a barrel which is bobbing through the rapids of a river. If that were not outrageous enough, the elf is simultaneously picking off orcs with his well-aimed arrows. A few scenes later, Bilbo enters the fearsome dragon's lair and proceeds to remove his ring. The dragon can see him several times, and yet never catches him. The dwarves also enter the mountain and are seen by the dragon who fails to dispatch them as well. The whole company dashes madly around the mountain passages narrowly escaping death multiple times. At one point Jackson even includes the preposterous scene of a dwarf riding through a molten metal river in a metal wheelbarrow to escape the clumsily portrayed dragon. As I mentioned before, the dwarves brought Bilbo on the journey to stealthily steal back their treasure from the dragon because no one could survive any other way, yet Jackson ignored this fact and instead saturated the movie with ludicrous occurrences. Most reviews of *The Hobbit: The Desolation of Smaug* praise the movie for being full of action. Richard Corliss in the article "The Hobbit: The Desolation of Smaug: It Lives!" heralds the production as an energetic, lively sequel (pars. 1-5). I reject such claims because the action is so unbelievable and repetitive that it becomes tiring to watch. Jackson cut out logical action from The Hobbit to replace it with thoughtless, melodramatic action.

The biggest problem with Peter Jackson's production of *The Hobbit: The Desolation of Smaug* was his infidelity to the theme of Tolkien's novel. Ultimately, Jackson could have altered the characters, the plot, and the action in the movie and not ruined it. He strayed when he changed the theme of the story. Tolkien's original work emphasized the development of the hobbit Bilbo. Tolkien's story throws Bilbo into a mix of circumstances that force him to become independent and to develop courage. This is proven by the climax of the book where Bilbo musters the courage to act alone and against his companions to ultimately save them from their own greed. Jackson missed the point and created different unfocused themes. He removed the spotlight from Bilbo's development. Instead of keeping the theme, the heart of Tolkien's book, Jackson created trite themes through the addition of characters and the deletion of key scenes that contained Tolkien's theme. Then Jackson glossed over the unfocused movie by filling the film with senseless action that bored viewers. When Jackson or any movie producer adapts a story to be film, he should always remain faithful to the theme of the tale because that is the heart of a tale.

Works Cited

Barsanti, Chris. "The Hobbit: The Desolation of Smaug." *Film Journal International* 117.1 (2014): 58-59. *Film &*

Television Literature Index with Full Text. Web. 14 Mar. 2014.

Corliss, Richard. "The Hobbit: The Desolation of Smaug: It Lives." *Time.* Time Inc., 9 Dec. 2013.*Academic Search Complete.* Web. 14 Mar. 2014.

Gleiberman, Owen. "The Hobbit: The Desolation of Smaug." *Entertainment Weekly* 20 Dec. 2013: 46. *Academic Search Complete.* Web. 14 Mar. 2014.

McCarthy, Todd. "The Hobbit: The Desolation of Smaug." *Hollywood Reporter* 419.45 (2013): 82-84.*Film & Television Literature Index with Full Text.* Web. 14 Mar. 2014.

The Hobbit: The Desolation of Smaug. Dir. Peter Jackson. Warner Bros. Entertainment Inc., 2013. Film.

Tolkien, J.R.R. *The Hobbit.* New York: Del Rey Books, 2012. Print.

"Genre's Definition Examined"
by Kayla Strasser

Instructor's Notes

In this paper, Kayla uses Rhetorical Genre Theory to give an extended definition of the term "genre." She uses that theory as the basis of an argument for the misrepresentation of the term "genre" within the general public, and why it is important for writers to have an accurate and complex understanding of what genres really are. She uses difficult, scholarly texts to support her claims about genre, and uses a high level of critical thinking to make a complex definition of genre. What is the argument she is actually making? Why is an extended definition considered an argument? What makes this such a complex argument?

Writer's Biography

Kayla Strasser is a freshman (class of 2017) Nursing major from Springfield, OH. Kayla enjoys reading and academic writing. She spends her free time with family and serving with her church. Her hobbies include working out, yard work and playing piano.

Genre's Definition Examined

Recently, genre scholars have tasked themselves with the complex assignment of defining genre. Scholars such as Lloyd Bitzer, Anis Bawarshi, Stanley E. Fish, and Amy Devitt have made consequential progress in defining genre and explaining how it is used in all facets of life. However, many people outside the compositional community grossly misunderstand genre, failing to realize its importance. Thus despite the illuminating efforts and research of genre scholars, some people remain unconvinced and insistently hold an erroneous view of genre. Drawing from the research of genre experts, this paper will dispel an erroneous understanding of genre and examine its actual definition. It will define genre as a fitting response to repetitive rhetorical situations, being defined by the reader's interpretation, and being flexible within its form.

A primary component of genre's definition is its response to a repeated rhetorical situation, which Bitzer defines as "a natural context of persons, events, objects, relations, and an exigence which strongly invites utterance" (5). Thus, a rhetorical situation is a condition that comes about through people, relationships, events, etc., which require some sort of oral or written response. For example, the death of a president creates a situation that requires a eulogy in response to the death. Upon further explanation of the response required by the situation, Bitzer states that "Rhetorical discourse comes into existence as a response to a situation, in the same sense that an answer comes into existence in response to a question, or a solution in response to a problem" (5). In essence, Bitzer is saying that a rhetorical situation is what brings genre into existence. Each rhetorical situation has an exigence, a need marked by urgency, which requires an apt response, just as the death of a president (the situation) requires a eulogy (the fitting response). As these situations are often repetitive, discourse communities have established specific, traditional, pragmatic and methodical responses to them. These fitting responses are genres. Thus, far from simply being a classification as some people might understandably argue "after all, the word genre, borrowed from the French, means "sort" or "kind" " (Bawarshi 7), genres are firstly, an appropriate response to a specific situation.

Having established that genres are fitting responses, it is then possible to refute another of the myths believed about genre's definition. Some people believe that genre is identified purely by its form. For example, Stanley Fish asks, "How do you recognize a poem when you see one? The commonsense answer, to which many literary critics and linguists are committed, is that the act of recognition is triggered by the observable presence of distinguishing features. That is, you know a poem when you see one because its language displays the characteristics that you know to be proper to poems" (para 6). However, genre is defined by the interpretation of the reader. Fish illustrates this by using an experiment he did on some of his students who were studying religious poetry as an example. He put up a random list of names on the board, told his students it was a poem, and instructed them to devise its meaning: which they did elaborately. Fish uses this example as evidence that literary works don't fit into genres because they follow the form of that genre. As he states, "The conclusion therefore is that all objects are made and not found, and that they are made by the interpretive strategies we set in motion" (para 24). By this he means that texts are placed into that genre by the interpretation of a discourse community. Fish's students were able to devise the meaning of that list of names because of how they interpreted it, not because it fit into a specific genre form.

Amy Devitt adds to the discussion of form/interpretation by stating that " I will argue not for teaching the textual features of particular genres...but rather for teaching genre awareness... as a side effect of teaching genre awareness, students may also acquire new genres that can serve as antecedent genres for their future writing" (192). Devitt is arguing for a learning strategy that echoes Fish's point about genres being defined by the reader's interpretation. Rather than teaching the very specific formulas of an individual genre, she proposes that students learn to interpret genre so that they can go anywhere that it exists and know how to learn and use that genre. Thus, despite the resolve with which many hold onto this mistaken understanding, genre is not defined by form, but rather by the interpretation of the reader.

One final fictitious belief held by some is that genre acts as an austere master that requires slavish obedience and conformity to the forms and formulas of that genre. This is simply not the case. Genres are evolving forms; not a rigid set of rules to which writers must adhere. Though all works are limited by genre and the work and worldview of earlier authors, as Bawarshi states, " rather than being static backdrops against which speakers and writers act, social and rhetorical conditions are constantly being reproduced and transformed as speakers and writers act within them" (9). In other words, genres build upon the work of earlier writers and evolve over time as they are used by diverse discourse communities with varying ideologies and purposes. From this, Devitt concludes that "Genres allow a range of choices, as well as set constraints" (200). Though writing will always be limited by the mere fact that genre exists, it also changes alongside the communities that use it, and is thus far from inflexible.

While current research, defining genre as a fitting response to repetitive rhetorical situations, being defined by the reader's interpretation, and being flexible within its form, has dispelled many erroneous beliefs about genre's definition, there is still room to grow. This topic is far from exhausted and perhaps, with further research, it may be possible to persuade those who continue to stubbornly hold on to mistaken views of genre.

Works Cited

Bawarshi, Anis. *Genre and the Invention of the Writer: Reconsidering the Place of Invention in Writing.* Logan: Utah State University Press, 2003. 7-9. Print.

Bitzer, Lloyd. "Rhetorical Situation". *Philosophy and Rhetoric.* 1992: Vol. 25, p1-14. 14p. Article.

Devitt, Amy. *Writing Genres.* Carbondale: Southern Illinois University Press, c2004. 192-200. Print.

Fish, Stanley. I*s There a Text in This Class?.* Cambridge: Harvard University Press, 1980. 6-24. Print.

"Occupational Therapists in the Field of Writing" by Meredith Merritt

Instructor's Notes

This essay has a dual purpose of providing a rhetorical analysis of a scholarly journal article and an overview of writing in the field of occupational therapy. Meredith Merritt successfully achieves both purposes. What organizational style(s) does she employ? After reading Meredith's essay, do you believe you have a good understanding of the kinds of writing occupational therapists complete? Can you name the article Meredith analyzes? What are her feelings toward the article? How do you know?

Writer's Biography

Meredith Merritt is a sophomore Allied Health major from Pennsylvania. She is currently preparing to enter the field of occupational therapy in the hopes of putting to good use her love for people. She enjoys a wide range of hobbies, from reading literature to carving down mountains on her snowboard. Her heart, however, remains firmly attached to working at summer church camps.

Occupational Therapists in the Field of Writing

When considering writers, many people may automatically think about authors, journalists, playwrights; they may associate writing with the forms they have personally encountered. This understanding based on exposure, however, overlooks different areas of writing that many people may have never before come across. For instance, while many may perceive occupational therapy as involving a more hands-on approach in working with patients, it actually encompasses a fair amount of writing as well. Such professionals may write on a daily, and sometimes even long-term, basis. While the daily type writings may include progress notes and/or evaluations, long-term and more extensive type works may consist of peer-reviewed research articles or other research-oriented projects. In producing each of these different pieces, occupational therapists find themselves writing for varying audiences, a task which mandates flexibility in writing style. As a whole, their job necessitates a skill level in writing that enables them to construct progress notes, evaluations, peer-reviewed articles, etc., in such a way as to concisely establish the relevancy and validity of their writing, while simultaneously maintaining an educational, formal tone. Masne Kadar, Rachael McDonald, and Primrose Lentin capture this skillset in an article they had published in the *Australian Occupational Therapy Journal.*

As with many occupations that interact with patients on a day-to-day basis, the writing of occupational therapists may manifest itself in many different forms. Beginning at the graduate level, prospective occupational therapists encounter a variety of writing projects, most of which usually develop from a research-oriented foundation. Although not identical in nature, physical therapists and occupational therapists often utilize similar forms of writing in their fields. According to Dr. Sled, a physical therapist and professor at Cedarville University, many of her graduate courses required the submission of papers, some types of which included research papers, critical appraisals, and research proposals. The common theme between all of these pieces lies in their reliance on research. Whether the piece presents new findings or analyzes the results of others, the research basis ultimately acts in enabling the field of occupational therapy to continue advancing at a rapid rate. Some other research-based items Dr. Sled recalled writing included applications for research grants, three ten-page papers on randomly assigned topics, and her graduate school thesis. Eventually, once out of graduate school, occupational therapists may contribute new ideas to this bank of research by conducting their own studies and publishing their findings in academic, peer-reviewed journals (Sled). Outside of these intense studies, clinical occupational therapists also constantly record daily progress notes during each patient's visit (Barbieri). In the case of Debra Barbieri, a practicing physical therapist in Virginia, her notes follow the pattern abbreviated as SOAP—subjective, objective, assessment, plan. To complete her report, she then develops an evaluation after working with and observing the individual. In general, the types of writing occupational therapists do often depends on the role they choose to pursue within the field.

Regardless of the end product, writing in this field requires the development and implementation of key skills that allow occupational therapists to effectively communicate findings, analyses, and evaluations. One such example is the 2012 academic research article entitled, "Evidence-based practice in occupational therapy services for children with autism spectrum disorders in Victoria, Australia," by Masne Kadar, Rachael McDonald, and Primrose Lentin. These researchers sought to simultaneously inform and persuade their audience—primarily occupational therapy practices—by carefully developing a highly structured article that addressed the need for change within the field. To begin with, they first captured the attention of the audience by explaining the relevancy and importance of their study: "Globally, the incidence of children diagnosed with autism spectrum disorder (ASD) has increased substantially over recent years" (284). They then built on this foundation by developing a strong sense of credibility. Unlike the implementation of ethos in more informal works of writing that might rely on developing voice, the authors of this article established ethos through strong supporting evidence from outside resources. In one particular instance, they remark, "This result [of professionals collaborating] is consistent with the finding from the Watling et al. (1999a) survey that occupational therapists regularly collaborate with other professionals during both the evaluation and intervention process" (290). Through statements such as these, Kadar, McDonald, and Lentin establish the legitimacy of their research, thereby enabling their audience to perceive it as truth.

In crafting this paper, the authors further develop their credibility through concise presentation of information. They present their material through a format closely resembling that of the scientific method. Broken into eight main categories, it includes the following headings: "Background," "Introduction," "Methods," "Results," "Discussion," "Conclusion," "Acknowledgments," and "References." This structure, including both data tables and written paragraph form, not only makes the paper easier to read and comprehend, but it also creates a concise, formal tone. With the titles and subtitles differentiating between sections, Kadar, McDonald, and Lentin avoid any unnecessary, wordy transitions. Each section merely discusses exactly that which its heading identifies. The results section in particular remains concise, presenting the findings without explanation: "A high number of participants (90.9%) reported that they used sensory processing or sensory integration assessments" (287). Eventually, in the "Discussion" and "Conclusion" sections, they do incorporate their interpretation of the results into the piece. However, they still elaborate only as far as enabled by their results. Within each of these formal elements, the authors also utilize a practice common to the scientific field as a whole—the use of passive voice. By making statements such as, "Environmental modifications have been identified as the interventions that are most likely to enable children with ASD to achieve success in their daily activities" (290), the authors remove the subject from the action performed. In part, this reliance on passive voice makes the writing style appear more objective. Therefore, by taking themselves out of the presentation of the results, the authors incorporate a seemingly unbiased voice into the concise format, all of which contributes to the development of ethos and to the overall strength of the paper.

As a whole, the authors of this article succeed in effectively contributing to the advancement of the field of occupational therapy. Through careful presentation of information, they maintain a high level of credibility. Additionally, by remaining mindful of the purpose of this specific type of writing, the authors remain concise and impartial. This reliability remains crucial to academic journals seeking to enable the progression of occupational therapy. Effective articles such as this often serve as the tools that guide occupational therapists in identifying better methods of treatment. Then, with this research in mind, evidence of an advancing field reveals itself through the progress notes clinical occupational therapists record as they implement these new methods of treatment. In a sense, writing in occupational therapy creates an interconnected cycle that propels the field forward.

Works Cited

Barbieri, Debra. Email interview. 2 Apr. 2014.

Kadar, Masne, Rachael McDonald, and Primrose Lentin. "Evidence-Based Practice in Occupational Therapy Services For Children With Autism Spectrum Disorders in Victoria, Australia." *Australian Occupational Therapy Journal* 59.4 (2012): 284-293. Web. 9 Apr. 2014.

Sled, Elizabeth. Email interview. 2 Apr. 2014.

"*A Separation* Builds a Connection"
by Rebecca Mangan

Instructor's Notes

In her research paper, Rebecca explores how cultural differences, although they initially appear to separate us, can actually be the starting points for building bridges. How might an author's presuppositions unfairly influence his or her conclusions when dealing with a foreign culture? How might one's own biases be identified, negotiated, and diminished? Why is this important? Is it possible for an outsider to a cultural group to speak about that group with authority? How might a writer/researcher create ethos to help establish authority?

Writer's Biography

Rebecca Mangan is a junior Nursing major who is passionate about diversity and views writing as a crucial tool in dissolving differences. In 2008, she traveled as a reporter with Y-Press to the Republican National Convention. Last year she won a national essay contest for Abercrombie and Fitch's diversity and inclusion campaign. During middle school and high school, Mangan published in her state newspaper, the Indianapolis Star, and spoke on NPR wfyi radio in Indianapolis. She searches for opportunities to glorify God with the gifts He has given and to serve others through them.

A Separation Builds a Connection

A Separation, an Iranian courtroom drama, opens with main characters Nader and Simin requesting a divorce before a judge. It appears their marriage has suffered for some time now as they wearily restate their reasons for separation. Simin is determined to leave Iran with Termeh, their 11-year-old daughter while Nader, loyal to his elderly father, refuses to leave. The judge prods—what is wrong with raising their daughter in Iran? Simin's answer is ambiguous, only replying that she doesn't want to raise Termeh under "these circumstances." The question of why the current state of Iran is bleak for an intelligent young daughter like Termeh is left unanswered. The subtleties in *A Separation* lead the viewer to wonder about the current struggle for gender equality in Iran today, after the Iranian Revolution of 1979 reversed efforts of egalitarianism. In order to interpret the subtleties of the film, one must understand the events in Iran that led up to its current turmoil: the White Revolution, the Iranian Revolution, and the current Women's Rights movement in modern Iran.

The White Revolution of 1963 led by Reza Shah Pahlavi was the culmination of efforts of women that started at the very beginning of the 20th century. In Iran during the 1800s, the majority believed that Iranian women did not need education apart from the knowledge necessary to raise children, manage a home, and honor the family name (Nashiravani). However, at the beginning of the 20th century, Iran could no longer stand at odds with the modernization of the rest of the world. Women were at the forefront leading this change, desiring education and equal opportunities for civic involvement. As a result, in 1906, schools opened by American missionaries and French immigrants allowed young girls to enroll and a year later, a society of both men and women formed to herald cross-gender political debate and discussion, encouraging women to be involved in sociopolitical matters. This society was called The Women's Freedom Society and later became The National Ladies' Society (Nashiravani).

When Reza Shah Pahlavi was crowned king in 1925 the progress accelerated. The dawn of the Pahlavi era was the harbinger of economic, social, and political reforms to make Iran a global power. This period of time is known as The White Revolution. The Shah realized that Iran could not join modern society if gender equality was not addressed (Wright). Reza Shah initiated four incredible changes in 1936. In the realm of education, both men and women were admitted to Tehran University. In the realm of politics, women obtained the right to vote and run for parliament. In the realm of family, women gained the right to petition for divorce and gain child custody, when in the past men could both declare divorce and take custody of children by default (Wright). Lastly, during the White Revolution, the Shah removed the mandatory chador for women.

After 1936, when Reza Shah banned the chador, veiling came to be perceived among the minority of elite and secular middle-class women as a symbol of oppression... Iranian society was already polarized between the traditionally minded majority and a minority of involved women who were dedicated to improving the status of women. (Curtis)

Because of The White Revolution, by 1978, "22 women sat in parliament and 333 women served on elected local councils. One-third of university students were female. Two million women were in the work force, more than 146,000 of them in the civil service" (Wright).

As a response, however, another revolution formed. This revolution of 1979 is known as "The Iranian Revolution," or sometimes, "The Islamic Revolution." During this time, Reza Shah Pahlavi was overthrown, in an attempt to combat the "liberalism" of previous years and reestablish fundamentals of Islam. The revolution was primarily lead by two theorists, Ayatollah Khomeini and Ali Shari'ati. "Shari'ati drew on a Shi'a model of womanhood to highlight women's central role as daughters, wives, and mothers" (Sameh). This model was a gentle way of pushing women out of positions of power and back into the kitchen and home. Both leaders were passionate about reversing the secularization that the Pahlavi era had brought and returning to Islamic tradition.

Khomeini gained an immense following and eventually gained enough influence to be the face of the revolution. Surprisingly, many women supported the revolution, being persuaded by Khomeini's charisma and desire to establish Iran's identity. He often said that under the Shah's regime, Iran was a "puppet of the United States" (Wright).

Haideh Moghissi, current Islam and Gender Project Director and founder of the Iranian National Union of Women, wrote in retrospect:

We had failed to listen carefully to Khomeini's rhetorical pronouncements that the new government would provide women with all rights denied to them, 'within the confines of the Shari'a [Islamic Law].' The meaning was crystal clear. However, the dominance of populist, anti-imperaialist tendencies or unrealistic expectations about the revolution within the ranks of the most active, gender-conscious sections of the female population—urban, educated, middle-class women—prevented us from seeing through the revolutionary promises and the Islamists' medieval agenda…(Moghissi 20)

Despite the Shah's efforts to silence Khomeini, even banishing him from Iran, Khomeini returned in 1979 and successfully overthrew the Shah. Khomeini was immediately recognized as the new leader of Iran, writing an Islamic constitution and being heralded the first "Supreme Leader." In his years as leader, he established the Islamic Republic of Iran.

As leader, he reversed almost all progress from the White Revolution. "The new theocracy systematically rolled back five decades of progress in women's rights. Women were purged from government positions. All females, including girls in first grade, were forced to observe the hijab, or Islamic dress code" (Wright). Furthermore, "After the victory of the revolution, women discovered that the revolution they thought they loved did not love them back, or value the advances women had made. Equality between men and women was not on the agenda of the Islamic Republic" (Esfandiari).

Today, in the circumstances movie character Simin alludes to, women still battle the damage that Khomeini's rule caused, despite many setbacks. "33 years after the revolution, Iranian women still have not regained their pre-revolutionary rights" (Esfandiari). Most the female activists were raised with the freedoms of the Pahlavi era. Francesco Bongioni, a journalist for the *New Yorker* interviewed activist Negin Ehtesabian, a 40-year-old artist in Tehran, and published an article about the circumstances through the eyes of an Iranian woman.

Today, the Islamic Republic's gender laws are among the harshest in the world. They penalize women in the areas of marriage, divorce, child custody, and inheritance. Polygamy is legal for men, and the legal testimony of one man carries the same weight as that of two women, an imbalance that helps explain why there are so few convicted rapists in Iran. Against this background, women like Negin—educated, cosmopolitan, and old enough to have come of age before the Islamic Revolution—occupy an anomalous position. They were formed in a society far more liberal, if not necessarily freer, than the one they now inhabit. And though Iranian women remain very highly educated by the standards of surrounding countries, the social and professional avenues open to them are often disappointingly narrow. (Bongiorni)

Though at first the Iranian Revolution appears to be devastating to all women's rights initiatives, many onlookers like journalist Bongiorni and author Catherine Sameh agree that the revolution made the women even more passionate today. Sameh writes, "It is in this post-revolutionary period, particularly in the last decade and a half, that women have emerged as key agents of many important changes in the social, political and cultural landscape of Iran" (Sameh 9). The attempts of the 1980s to silence women caused even more energy in the women's movement, leaving Iran with one of the most charged and dynamic women's movements in the Islamic world. Many female activists involved have won international recognition (Wright).

Along with the constant actions specific to women's rights, a new school of thought is forming called "Islamic Modernism." This viewpoint tries to reconcile Islamic faith with modern values, incorporating democracy, civil rights, and equality, and creating a new version of the Islamic faith (Moaddel 2). In addition to agreeing with the need for gender equality, the viewpoint removes Islamic supremacist tendencies and seeks to live at peace with other faiths. If Islamic Modernism becomes popular thought, Iran may return to a state of progress similar to its pre-revolution state. Daniel Pipes, president of the Middle East Forum, who is optimistic about the modernization of Iran, summarizes, "This synthesis would choose among Shari precepts and render Islam compatible with modern values. It would accept gender equality, coexist peacefully with unbelievers, and reject the aspiration of a universal caliphate, among other steps" (Pipes).

In conclusion, *A Separation* effectively leads the viewer to wonder about the current circumstances in Iran and the preceding events that led to the turmoil. A thorough understanding of the White Revolution led by Reza Shah, the Iranian Revolution led by Ayatollah Kohmeini, and the current state of gender roles in Iran, give context to the subtleties of *A Separation*. Simin's ambiguous answer in the courtroom left the viewer to question what "circumstances" in Iran fueled her desire to flee the country with her daughter Termeh. When *A Separation* was the first Iranian film to win an Academy Award for Best Foregin Language Film, director Asghar Farhadi had successfully built a connection from American viewers to modern Iran. By creating Simin, Farhadi gave a face and name to an Iranian woman living with the struggle in Tehran yet delivered this message subtly enough to allow the movie to be released. In a review of the film, Azar Nafisi, the author of *Reading Lolita in Tehran: a Memoir in Books*, says:

> The most important aspect of Iran is the people that have always, in fact, resisted their oppression—not just with protests, but also by continuing to live the way they lived before the regime. A movie like A Separation brings out that same aspect of Iran, the human aspect. When you see a film like A Separation, you realize not how different Americans are from the Iranian regime, but how similar they are to the Iranian people. (Hayoun)

Works Cited

Bongiorni, Francesco. "Veiled Threat." *New Yorker* 85.31 (2009): 38-43. Literary Reference Center. Web. 2 Dec. 2013

Curtis, Glenn E., and Eric J. Hooglund. *Iran: A Country Study.* 5th ed. Washington, DC: Library of Congress, Federal Research Division, 2008. Print.

Esfandiari, Haleh. "For Women Of The Arab Spring, Iranian Women Provide A Warning And A Model." *Turkish Policy Quarterly* 11.4 (2012): 81-89. *Political Science Complete.* Web. 2 Dec. 2013.

Hayoun, Massoud. "The Atlantic." *The Atlantic.* The Atlantic Monthly Group, 15 Feb. 2012. Web. 02 Dec. 2013.

Moaddel, Mansoor. *Islamic Modernism, Nationalism, and Fundamentalism: Episode and Discourse.* Chicago: University of Chicago, 2005. Print.

Moghissi, Haideh. "Arab Uprisings and Women's Rights: Some Lessons from Iran." *Against The Current.* 28.3 (2013): 18-22. *Academic Search Complete.* Web. 2 Dec. 2013

Nashiravani, Reyhaneh. "Iranian Women in the Era of Modernization: A Chronology." Foundation for Iranian Studies. Foundation for Iranian Studies, 25 Aug. 2009. Web. 01 Dec. 2013.

Pipes, Daniel. "Can Islam Be Reformed?." Commentary 136.1 (2013): 31-34.Literary Reference Center. Web. 2 Dec. 2013.

Sameh, Catherine. "Still In The Street: Three Decades Of Iranian Women's Activism." *Against The Current* 24.4 (2009): 8-10. Academic Search Complete. Web. 2 Dec. 2013.

Wright, Robin B. *The Iran Primer: Power, Politics, and U.S. Policy.* Washington, D.C.: United States Institute of Peace, 2010. Print.

"The Professional Woman's Journey"
by Casey Morrone

Instructor's Notes

In this essay, Casey Morrone responds to Virginia Woolf's essay, Professions for Women. Casey effectively achieves her purpose for this essay by writing a thesis that applies Woolf's message to a current context. What do you think works well in this essay? What could be improved upon and how?

Writer's Biography

Casey Morrone, a native New Yorker, is a Molecular and Cellular Biology major pursuing a career in medicine. She has a penchant for exploring new places and daydreaming about different cities she'd like to live in one day. Casey finds enjoyment in a broad range of activities including her current job as a resident assistant, watching football, and appreciating art of all sorts--spanning from literature to fashion.

The Professional Woman's Journey

In today's modern era, the conversation about women's rights and feminism is in vogue. Like the latest must-have item in fashion, feminism is the garment that everyone is eager to slip into. Feminism and women's rights are currently being applied to a wealth of different situations. The topic of women in the workplace, however, can be traced all the way back to the beginning of the 20th century, if not further. In fact, Virginia Woolf spoke of the barriers that women faced in their newfound professions, such as writing, back in 1931. In her speech from which the essay *Professions for Women* is derived, Woolf addressed both specific and abstract challenges that women faced in the professional environment, especially the environment of writing. In the modern day, some of these challenges have been conquered, some still remain obstacles, and others still have not yet been identified but oppose professional women all the same.

When Virginia Woolf gave her speech, women had only begun to choose occupations for themselves outside the home. It is no secret that, prior to this time, a woman's place was viewed to be in the home rather than in the workplace with a career. She was supposed to put everyone else's needs above her own. Although times were changing, this image of women pervaded. This explains the existence of the first obstacle that Woolf exposed: "The Angel in the House" (Woolf, 2005, P. 349)[1]. She described the Angel in the House as a "phantom" who was "intensely sympathetic," "immensely charming," and "utterly unselfish." She "excelled in the difficult arts of family life" and "sacrificed herself daily." Furthermore, she "preferred to sympathize always with the minds and wishes of others" rather than have "a mind or wish of her own" and—most importantly—was "pure" (P. 349-350). The Angel in the House appears to be none other than the ideal, turn-of-the-century housewife. This phantom of outdated values "bothered" and "tormented" Woolf to such a great extent that she "turned upon her and caught her by the throat" (P. 350). "Had I not killed her she would have killed me," Woolf reasoned in "self-defense" (P. 350). Through vivid and dramatic descriptions, Woolf made it clear that the Angel in the House was no longer an obstacle that women in her day need face. The idea of what a woman should be and should do was shifting, and the phantom was being trampled in the process. Whereas the women in Woolf's day battled with the phantom, women in the modern age have undoubtedly never experienced such a phantom. Nowadays women are encouraged to develop dreams and goals for their lives and to take the necessary steps to accomplish them. It can be argued that the modern woman is the antithesis of the Angel in the House. Clearly, professional women today do not face the challenge of the Angel in the House.

The second challenge that Woolf addressed was one that was more specific to women in the profession of writing than to women in other professions, but the barrier it created was significant nonetheless. According to Woolf, female writers had to overcome the challenge of "telling the truth about [their] own experience[s] as [bodies]" (P. 352). In Woolf's day, it was "unfitting for her as

---

1 The rest of the citations in this essay refer to Virginia Woolf's speech-turned-essay, Professions for Women, which was edited by Jane E. Aaron and published in 40 Model Essays: A Portable Anthology in 2005.

a woman" to speak or write "about the body, about the passions" as men did (P. 352). Woolf expressed that "men sensibly [allowed] themselves great freedom in these respects" but "[condemned] such freedom in women" (P. 352). Unlike the last obstacle Woolf addressed in her speech, she did not feel as though she, nor any female writer, had conquered this one, but that was eighty years ago. Today, this obstacle has indeed crumbled at the feet of female writers. The stigma that existed for women in Woolf's day is nowhere to be found. It has become acceptable for women to write about whatever they choose. However, while this barrier is no longer in place for female writers, women still fight a losing battle with the passions. This is evident in the attitudes towards promiscuity, adultery, and the like. A woman found guilty of one of these things is typically judged more harshly and viewed more critically than a man would be in the same circumstance. This trend does not exclude the workplace, which potentially leaves professional women susceptible to unequal treatment when compared to male colleagues. This is one example of how the barrier mentioned by Woolf has morphed and continues to torment women in their professions.

Woolf considered writing to be "the freest of all professions for women," yet she still encountered obstacles in her professional experiences (P. 352). Acknowledging this, she addressed the "ghosts" and "prejudices" that women faced in "the new professions which [they] are now for the first time entering" (P. 352). She suggested that "the obstacles against [professional women] are still immensely powerful—and yet they are very difficult to define" (P. 352). This is one assertion that holds just as true today as it did in Woolf's day.

In the decades since Woolf gave her speech, women have infiltrated just about every occupation. Women can be found prosecuting in court, serving in Congress, fighting in the military, performing surgery in the operating room, selling stocks on Wall Street, announcing sporting events on live television, researching cures for terminal diseases in the laboratory, or sitting behind a fancy desk at a large corporation—and not always as a secretary or assistant, either. Modern day women have no problem gaining access to whichever field of work they desire to pursue. This does not mean, however, that women have eliminated all of the obstacles opposing them in their professional endeavors. In more than a few cases, women still earn less than men do. Pay gaps have not decreased as expected over the years, especially in the medical field. On average, a physician makes around fifty thousand dollars more per year if birthed with a Y chromosome instead of a second X. As for the women behind the desk, they often feel the presence of a glass ceiling that prevents them from being promoted to executive positions in their companies. Despite all the women in the workforce, the reality is that the upper echelons of the corporate world are filled almost exclusively with men. One must ask the question, what exactly is the underlying obstacle—or perhaps, obstacles—that prevent women from equal standing with their male counterparts in the professional world? Like Woolf claimed eighty years ago, "they are very difficult to define" (P. 352). She believed that "Even when the path is nominally open—when there is nothing to prevent a woman from being a doctor, a lawyer, a civil servant—there are many phantoms and obstacles…looming her way" (P. 352-353). It is incredible how correct she was.

Speaking of the "phantoms and obstacles" still hindering women, Woolf stated that "To discuss and define them is…of great value and importance; for thus only can the labour be shared, the difficulties be solved" (P. 353). She raised an excellent point. Society should be participating in an active conversation that tries to define these obstacles. One of the first topics that should be addressed in such a discussion is this: perhaps a phantom still torments women. Yes, the Angel in the House died at the hand of professional women almost a century ago, but a new, modern day phantom seems to have taken her place. Birthed by a society that tells women that they can have it all, this phantom is the woman who has everything. She works a full time job, raises her children, has a good relationship with her husband, is involved in her community, and still manages to shop, clean, cook, and put dinner on the table for her family at six o'clock every night. This phantom eagerly accuses professional women everywhere. A woman who takes time off from work to raise her children is accused of not giving her full potential to her career; however, a woman who hires a nanny to raise her children while working full time is accused of neglecting her family by ranking her career as a higher priority. This creates an environment in which women are branded as inferior if they cannot measure up to the nearly impossible standard set by society. This modern day phantom is suffocating women and she must not be allowed to continue in her

73

devastating efforts. It is time for this phantom to be "caught...by the throat" and killed by women everywhere (P. 350).

But how does one go about killing this phantom? Women must pause and ask themselves why they as individuals are fighting to have everything. It doesn't come as a surprise that Woolf suggested this in her speech. After she charged women to "discuss and define" the barriers that hinder them in their professions, she continued by saying, "But besides this, it is necessary also to discuss the ends and the aims for which we are fighting, for which we are doing battle with the formidable obstacles. Those aims cannot be taken for granted; they must be perpetually questioned and examined" (P. 353). Therefore, in the name of evaluating ends and aims, it is not only time for the modern day phantom to reach her demise, but it is also time to reevaluate the proposition that women can have it all. Perhaps this claim is simply not true for some women, or maybe even for all women. Each woman needs to determine this for herself, however, as she decides what she—and not society—wants her life to look like. Women will ultimately be happier and more fulfilled if they are honest with themselves and form their goals accordingly because behind every female professional is a woman—a valuable human being who does not need to be defined by society's overwhelming expectations any more than women in Woolf's day needed to be defined by the Angel in the House.

Defining the obstacles, examining goals, and determining solutions will neither be easy nor come quickly. It certainly didn't for Virginia Woolf and her female peers. It is all worth it, however, if it means that women can be satisfied and unhindered in whatever path in life they choose.

Works Cited

Woolf, V. (2005). Professions for Women. In J. E. Aaron, *40 Model Essays: A Portable Anthology* (pp. 348-353). Boston: Bedford/St. Martin's.

Research Papers

Argumentitive
Persuasive
Expository
Position
Problem/Solution

"Single-Sex Versus Coeducation" by Kaitlyn Morse and Kelsey Gentry

Instructor's Notes

Kaitlyn Morse and Kelsey Gentry's argumentative synthesis demonstrates how effectively freshmen can collaborate on a research project. These students' paper represents the attentiveness to detail, thoroughness of research, and thoughtful consideration of opposing viewpoints this type of persuasive essay requires. It also meets its intended audience of scholars and sensitively negotiates the complexities educators and their students face in regards to this topic. What do you conclude after reading this essay? Think about what does, or doesn't, convince you. What do you find to be the most effective part of the paper? The least effective? Why?

Writers' Biography

Kaitlyn Morse is a junior Early Childhood Education major from Connecticut. She enjoys academic and non-academic writing and loves to read.

Kelsey Gentry is a sophomore Biology major from Virginia. She has enjoyed writing since early elementary school, particularly poems. Her other areas of interest include playing piano, sketching, hiking, and photography.

Single-Sex Versus Coeducation

If one takes an English phrase and translates it over and over into different languages, by the time one translates the phrase back into English, the result will differ completely from the original. This example is similar to what happens with much of the research behind single-sex education. Prominent scholars publish research, but by the time the research reaches the principal's desk, the teacher's hand, and the parent's newsletter, enthusiasts of single-sex schooling have distorted much of the original information. As a result, those who are in charge of the schools have ideas about single-sex education that may not be accurate. They hear wonderful things: that single-sex schools raise test scores, close the gender gap, or teach to children's set neurological needs. These ideas, of course, sound fantastic, but before parents, schools, and communities spend time and funds separating their children by gender, it might be wise to question the purported beliefs about single-sex education. In truth, it appears that single-sex educational schools are no more effective than coeducational schools, and since any value added has little to do with set gender or neurological differences between boys and girls, the uncertain legality and high cost of establishing a single-sex school cannot be justified.

A common assumption about single-sex education is that the gender composition of the schools contributes to the academic success of the attending students. However, as researchers delve deeper into the causes of academic success, they are finding that gender may not be one of the major contributors to academic success or failure. Rather, some studies conclude that other factors such as race and peer preferences influence a student's academic ability more than gender does.

One such study, conducted by Amy Roberson Hayes, Erin Pahlke, and Rebecca Bigler, explores the relationship between success in a single-sex school and factors such as peer preferences and selection of students. In the study, researchers compared the standardized test scores of girls attending a public, single-sex school with the scores of those attending a public, coeducational school, and the scores of those who applied to the single-sex school but were not accepted, and therefore ended up attending a public, coeducational school as well (Hayes, Pahlke, and Bigler 694). The results showed that girls attending the single-sex school had higher overall performance than those attending the coeducational school (701). However, when factors of school-driven selection and peer quality are taken into account, a whole new perspective arises.

According to Hayes, Pahlke, and Bigler, selection effects are one factor that researchers largely overlooked in previous studies of this nature (695). In general, it appears that the success rates of students attending single-sex schools are likely to be affected by two kinds of selection preferences (695). Firstly, there may be systematic differences, such as student motivation and scholastic achievement, between students who choose to enroll in a single-sex school and students who enroll in a coeducational school (695). Secondly, school-driven bias differentiates between students whose applications are accepted by administrators and students whose applications are rejected (695). These selection effects, in turn, greatly contribute to the quality of the students attending each school, whether they show high performance or low performance, which would in turn affect the test score outcomes. This study also takes peer quality into consideration. As noted before with selection effects, peer quality would largely depend on the type of school. In general, private schools have more finances at their disposal and higher academic standards than public schools. As such, comparing coeducational public schools to single-sex private schools is inaccurate, because the quality of the students will be different in each school. Based on the results of their study, which does take selection and peer quality factors into account, Hayes, Pahlke, and Bigler concluded that "it is overall peer quality, rather than the gender composition of the schools, that explains single-sex school students' outperformance of coeducational school students" (702).

Meagan Patterson and Erin Pahlke conducted a similar study that goes even further by examining the effects of factors such as race, prior academic achievement, and peer preferences. The data gathered during their study indicates that race definitely influences academic success. For instance, Patterson and Pahlke concluded from their study that African American and Latino students were more prone to lower grades than their peers of different ethnicities (746). Previous research has indicated that the academics of minority groups within a school are affected by the percentage of students of that minority in the school (746). Next, Patterson and Pahlke hypothesized that whatever academic achievement a student showed before attending a single-sex school would be an indicator of the student's achievement in the future (740). In accordance with their hypothesis, their results indicated that prior academic achievement does indeed predict future academic achievement (747).

The study also examines the factor of peer preference. Peer preference differs from peer quality, mentioned in the previous study, in that peer quality concerns the overall performance level of the students, while peer preference concerns the students' inclination towards male or female friends. Patterson and Pahlke hypothesized that peer preference would be a predictor of academic performance and persistence at a single-sex school (740). Their results indicated that students' gender preference in friends had an influence on whether or not they would remain at the school (747). However, these preferences did not necessarily have an effect on academic achievement (741). Peer preferences did, however, play a role in whether or not a student would remain at the single-sex school, which may or may not contribute to the school's success (748).

Given the results of these studies, the question remains as to whether single-sex schools are really more beneficial than coeducational schools. In general, the test scores of students attending single-sex schools are higher than those of students attending coeducational schools, so the question remains as to whether the overall success still remains higher when student and school factors are weighed in. According to an article by Diane Halpern et al. when it comes to single-sex schooling any "apparent advantages dissolve when outcomes are corrected for pre-existing differences" (1706). Therefore, simply taking standardized test scores from a single-sex school and comparing them with scores from a coeducational school is not accurate. As seen in previous studies, the scores from a single-sex school are generally higher than those from a coeducational school. However, when factors of selection, peer quality, race, prior academic achievement, and peer preferences are weighed in, the results may even out. Therefore, the results show no real differences between the schools. Also in need of consideration are any neurological differences that may have an effect on learning capabilities of girls versus boys.

Though advocates of single-sex education say that there are distinct differences between boys and girls, much of the research is neither applicable to children nor representative of the field of neuroscience. For example, in *Why Gender Matters,* Dr. Leonard Sax, a well-known advocate of single-sex education, talks about Virginia Technical School's study on 508 boys and girls, who were anywhere from two months to sixteen years in age. In his review and application of the study, Sax says that different areas of the brain, specifically those involved in spatial and verbal tasks, mature at different rates according to gender. According to him, girls are six years ahead of boys in fine motor skills, but boys are four years ahead of girls in spatial abilities (93).

However, as Dr. Lise Eliot points out, Sax probably

81

misinterpreted the data. To follow Sax's line of reasoning would be to say that one "cannot expect first-grade girls to learn their shapes or boys to begin reading and writing" (366). Not only did the study fail to test the brains while the children were involved in mental tasks, but also the data from the Virginia Tech study actually found "a cyclic pattern of maturation, with spurts of development that appeared to spiral through different brain areas" (366). This means that at the end of sixteen years, which was the oldest age in the study, boys' brains and girls' brains were equally mature in all areas. Also, at every point during the study there were significant differences within the two genders, as well as between them. Furthermore, as Eliot points out, the verbal capacity of two-year-old girls is only about a month ahead of that of two-year-old boys. Therefore, any differences in performance could not be based on brain maturation. This gap in capacity rises throughout preschool, but around age seven the differences become almost nonexistent (366). Sax used Virginia Technical School's study to make generalizations, saying that every boy and every girl will mature in the same way as all of his or her same-gender peers. In reality, children are different, even within their gender, and their minds are just as unique as they are. Some boys may be well ahead in mathematics, but the same could be true for some girls.

Another idea propagated by proponents of single-sex education states that boys and girls use different areas of their brains for similar tasks. For example, Michael Gurian, a prominent author in single-sex circles, and Kathleen Stevens authored *Boys and Girls Learn Differently*; in their book, they say that boys primarily use the right sides of their brains, but girls mainly use the left. Moreover, they state that "[b]oys tend to process emotive information from the limbic system to the brain stem . . . [whereas] girls tend to process it more in the upper brain, where complex thought occurs" (57). One should note that Gurian and Stevens list no citations to back their statements, and therefore the reader has to take their word.

Sax agrees with Gurian and Stevens, and cites a study of verbal IQ to prove his point. In the study, which looked at the brains of men and women after they suffered a stroke, the researchers found that men suffered the greatest drop in verbal IQ, about twenty percent, when the stroke affected their left hemisphere. There was not drop, however, when their right hemisphere suffered a stroke.

Women, on the other hand, had a near equal decrease, no matter which side was affected by the stroke (12). Based on this research, one might think that boys and girls process information differently; after all, the stroke affected the different genders in different ways. This may not be the case, however. As Eliot points out, "children's brains do not operate like adults: they are works-in-progress, and much of what influences adult neural circuitry is an individual's social- educational experience from birth until adulthood" (364). Therefore, since the research that Sax cites is based on studies that were done on adults, the research is not necessarily applicable to children or solid evidence in favor of single-sex education. Even if information is processed on different sides, it's clear that boys do not have "verbal barriers" that necessitate their separation from girls simply because of their gender, as some claim; their brains can process language just as easily as girls' can.

Moreover, though boys tend to do better in math and girls tend to do better in English, that fact is not necessarily a result of gender or the make-up of their brains. Achievement in different areas may instead be the result of a conglomeration of other factors, including the fact that little girls are encouraged to read for fun, and little boys are more likely to be encouraged to work off energy through sports. The activities they take part in when they are young translate into their interests and abilities once they are old enough to begin school. Furthermore, once children begin school, outside pressures tell them to conform to what society deems as normal for their gender (Jackson 228). Often times, especially during the pre-teen years, boys and girls settle into these patterns in order to fit in or to avoid being bullied because they are different. Therefore, it is not unreasonable to say that one of the reasons that each gender tends to do better in certain areas has at least as much to do with environment as it does with gender. Again, it should be noted that children are all different, and it is not fair to expect them to do well or poorly because of their gender. Such expectations might become self-fulfilling prophecies and keep children from doing their best with their natural talents and inclinations.

On top of the fact that there are no proven differences between boys and girls, the legality of establishing single-sex schools or classrooms is uncertain, and creating a single-sex school, or even single-sex classes, may result in lawsuits. The amendment to

Title IX was designed to "[allow] for single-sex schools *if* the school can show that the single-sex program was designed to overcome past gender discrimination" (Brown 358); however, many think that separating children based on gender is a form of discrimination. The American Civil Liberties Union (ACLU) has filed many lawsuits on behalf of families and communities that feel wronged or offended by the establishment of single-sex schools or classrooms in their district. Christina Brown, Ph.D., discusses one example, a lawsuit between Beckenridge County Middle School and the ACLU.

Starting in 2003, Beckenridge initiated gender segregation in math and science classes, but by 2004, they had created single-sex classes for almost every relevant subject, including the four core classes: math, history, science, and English (360). The middle school teachers also began teaching boys and girls differently, doing things such as playing reviews games with the boys but only quizzing the girls or letting boys be loud in class while girls were instructed to be quiet (360). The schools probably thought they were inside the boundaries of the law, but they had made several mistakes, including not allowing the parents a choice on single-sex or coeducation. After the classes had been implemented, the school sent a letter to the parents, but not all the parents received it. Parents complained and, together with the ACLU, sued the school (360-361). This short case study shows that implementing single-sex education can be risky for schools because of the large margin for error; if even one person does not know the laws, the entire school can be sued.

In addition to numerous influential outside factors, the lack of neurological differences, and the legal problems that come with establishing single-sex schools, it seems that there is simply not enough solid evidence to claim that gender separation in single-sex schools is the source of student success. In fact, according to Halpern et al. "there is no empirical evidence that [students'] success stems from their [single-sex] organization, as opposed to the quality of the student body, demanding curricula, and many other features also known to promote achievement at coeducational schools" (1706). Without evidence, one cannot justify the costs and effort needed to start and run a single-sex school. To start a public, single-sex school requires more teachers, classrooms, and funds than most school districts have available. Also, in order to offer single-sex education, school districts have to make co-educational schools available. This means that starting a single-sex school could greatly increase the budget that the district needs in order to keep their schools running. Therefore, as noted by Hayes, Pahlke and Bigler, costs and benefits of separation of students according to gender should be examined carefully before undertaking such a project.

In the end, little scientific evidence favoring single-sex schools actually exists, and the evidence that does exist is often mixed or inconclusive (Hayes, Pahlke, and Bigler 693). Most studies either do not take into account peer quality and other student characteristics, or show little or no difference in the schools once those factors are weighed in. Hayes, Pahlke, and Bigler add that "nearly all reviews cite design flaws, especially the possible presence of selection effects, as significantly hindering the interpretation of existing studies" (693). The article by Halpern et al. talks specifically about the lack of evidence in support of the benefits of single-sex schooling as an alternative to coeducational schooling (1706). In other words, gender itself does not appear to be the main determiner of students' success; therefore, the logical conclusion is that the high cost of establishing single-sex schools is not worth the uncertainty of the schools' success. Single-sex education limits self-discovery and forces children to miss out on friendships with, and the insight of, the opposite gender. Coeducation, on the other hand, allows children to start learning how to function in the real world, a world where men and women have to work together every single day.

Works Cited

Brown, Christia. "Legal Issues Surrounding Single-Sex Schools In The U.S.: Trends, Court Cases, And Conflicting Laws." *Sex Roles* 69.7/8 (2013): 356-362. Web. 17 Oct. 2013.

Eliot, Lise. "Single-Sex Education And The Brain." Sex Roles 69.7/8 (2013): 363-381.*Ebscohost*. Web. 22 Oct. 2013.

Gurian, Michael, and Kathy Stevens. *Boys and Girls Learn Differently!: A Guide for Teachers and Parents*. 3rd ed. San Francisco: Jossey-Bass, 2011. Web.

Halper, Diane, Lise Eliot, Rebecca Bigler, Richard Fabes, Laura Hanish, Janet Hyde, Lynn Liben, and Carol Martin. "The Pseudoscience of Single-Sex Schooling." *Sciencemag. org*. American Association for the Advancement of Science,

23 Sept. 2011. Web. 19 Nov. 2013.

Hayes, Amy, Erin Pahlke, and Rebecca Bigler. "The Efficacy of Single-Sex Education: Testing for Selection and Peer Quality Effects." *Sex Roles* 65.9 (2011): 693-703. *Ebscohost.* Web. 29 Oct. 2013.

Jackson, Janna. "'Dangerous Presumptions': How Single-Sex Schooling Reifies False Notions Of Sex, Gender, And Sexuality." Gender & Education 22.2 (2010): 227-238. *Ebscohost.* Web. 22 Oct. 2013.

Sax, Leonard. *Why Gender Matters: What Parents and Teachers Need to Know about the Emerging Science of Sex Differences.* New York: Doubleday, 2005. Print.

Patterson, Meagan, and Erin Pahlke. "Student Characteristics Associated with Girls' Success in a Single-Sex School." Sex Roles 65.9 (2011): 737-750. *Ebscohost.* Web. 29 Oct. 2013.

"Reaching for the Right Answer"
by Hannah Gaitan

Instructor's Notes

When writing an argument, students often believe contention or even aggression are required, but good rhetorical strategy requires the opposite. It requires knowing exactly who one's audience is and discerning ways to create unity with the audience, fostering respect, before accentuating differences. Aristotle identified this as an art – the art of persuasion – to be practiced and finessed, as opposed to verbal mud slinging. In this very well written argument, who do you think Hannah Gaitan's audience is? What strategies does she use to create unity and show respect for her audience. Can you point to specific word choices that achieve artful persuasion?

Writer's Biography

Hannah Gaitan is a second-year Pre-veterinary Medicine major from Boulder, Colorado. Hannah enjoys scientific writing, specifically dealing with animals, but finds creative writing and poetry to be difficult. She spends most of her time, however, studying for her classes and gaining hands on experience in the field of veterinary medicine. Her hobbies include equestrian sports, running, and hiking. She also enjoys hanging out with her family, boyfriend, and black lab, Buddy.

Reaching for the Right Answer

Introduction

Leaning up against the fence, smelling the fresh alfalfa, and listening to the soothing sound of the animals munching are the childhood memories I cherish the most. Ever since I was a child, I have loved to go to the zoo. To this day, I still sit and marvel at the beautiful creatures. Because of my deep love and passion for animals, I am working on a Biology degree at Cedarville University with an emphasis on Pre-Veterinarian medicine. Not only do I have a deep passion for animals, but I am fascinated by the science behind them. They each have their own unique traits and features working perfectly together to enable them to do magnificent things. Although I love to study and learn about all animals, the particular animal that strikes my interest is the giraffe. The giraffe towers over all the other mammals on earth. Because of its long neck and tall legs, the giraffe's heart must be extremely strong in order to pump the blood up the carotid artery (the artery that carries blood to the head) and to the giraffe's brain, supplying it with oxygen and nutrients (Zhang, 2006). Since the giraffe's head is so far away from its heart, the giraffe has hypertension, commonly known as high blood pressure. As a result of this hypertension, the giraffe contains many unique mechanisms that counteract the high blood pressure and keep the giant beast alive (Zhang, 2006). For example, the *rete mirable*, or "marvelous net," is a spongy mass of blood vessels located under the base of the brain that stretches gently to decrease the powerful force of the blood entering the brain (Pittman, 2011). This is just one of the mechanisms the giraffe possess and relies on for survival. As one may notice about the giraffe, it is not like any other mammal on this earth. Because of the giraffe's unique long neck and legs, scientists, through the years, have continually debated on how the giraffe obtained these features. There are generally two distinctive sides to this argument, Evolution and Creation. The people who support the Evolution theory are generally called Evolutionists. They are usually atheists, people who do not believe in a higher being. Evolutionists believe in Evolution, which is the change in inherited characteristics, enhancing the organism and making it more complex over an extensive period of time. The opposing side is Creationism which is usually argued by people termed Creationists. This group of people is frequently religious and believes in a god or designer. Creationists believe that a higher power, God, created organisms out of nothing and designed them with a purpose. Many Evolutionists and Creationists argue over the origin of the long neck of the giraffe. Evolutionists believe the giraffe's neck started out short and slowly evolved into the neck it is today. However, Creationists believe the giraffe's neck was made with a specific, intelligent design in mind and was created the same length as it is today. In this paper, I will explain both theories; however, the giraffe's neck was created long due to the evidence shown in the fossil record, the essential mechanisms in place because of high blood pressure, and the birthing process of a baby giraffe.

The Evolutionist's Theory

The giraffe (*Giraffa camelopardalis*) did not originally possess a long neck. Evolutionists believe the giraffe developed its long neck over an extensive period of time, about 50 million years. According to Evolutionists, the giraffe's neck evolved as a result of one or two possibilities (Simons & Altwegg, 2010). The first hypothesis is that the giraffe's neck evolved in order for the early giraffe species to compete against other browsers. This hypothesis was first presented in *The Descent of Man and Selection in Relation to Sex,* written by Darwin in 1871 (Simmons & Altwegg, 2010). Evolution of the short neck into a long neck would benefit the giraffe and allow it to graze for foliage which competitors could not reach ("competing browsers hypothesis") (Simons & Altwegg, 2010).

The second hypothesis is the "necks-for-sex" hypothesis. According to Simons and Altwegg (2010) the giraffe's neck evolved "for direct use in intra-sexual combat" in order to gain a mate. Evolutionists believe the giraffe's short neck gradually evolved into a longer neck through the process of a certain genes being passed down to the offspring. According to Simmons and Altwegg (2010) who cite Pratt and Anderson (1985), Brand (2007), and Darwin (1871) there are many lines of evidence which support the "necks for sex" hypothesis. First, the males with the longer and larger necks are the males which have the greatest chance of winning a female. Second, the female giraffes prefer males with larger necks. Third, "sexual traits are usually positively allometric [relative growth of a part (the neck) in relation to an entire organism (the giraffe)] (Simmons & Altwegg, 2010). Since the long neck is viewed as a sexual trait, males which successfully breed with the females due to their longer necks will pass this trait along from generation to generation over millions of years, thus resulting in a giraffe with a long neck. These two hypotheses both explain why the giraffe's neck evolved from a short to long.

Evolutionists admit to some problems with their hypotheses. According to Simons and Altwegg (2010), studies made by Simons & Scheepers (1996) "[were] found to [have] inconsistent support from foraging studies" (p. 7). Recent studies by Shorrocks in 2009 showed the giraffe frequently grazed at shoulder length and below during the winter when the food would be most scarce. Simons & Scheepers cited Young and Isbell (1991) who researched and found that giraffes actually feed quicker at shoulder level. South African giraffes, however, were found to graze more often on plants higher then shoulder level (Simmons & Altwegg, 2010). It was determined these giraffes grazed at higher levels because the proper forage was located higher during the winter months (Simmons & Altwegg, 2010). The first hypothesis is threatened by one result and supported by another.

According to Simmons and Atlwegg (2010), "The sexual selection hypothesis predicts neutral selection on females and positive selection on males" (p. 7). This is one of the challenges the second hypothesis faces. The problem Evolutionists admit to is that natural selection should affect both genders, but sexual selection only accounts for the males' long necks. Simmons and Altwegg (2010) state that there is a need to explain "why female giraffes also have long necks" (p. 11). These are the two hypotheses Evolutionists present in order to explain the giraffe's long neck.

The Creationist's Theory

Creation argument is the counter argument to the Evolution argument. According to Dr. Elizabeth Mitchell (2013), who has studied chemistry and practiced medicine, "Biblical history informs us that God created all kinds of land animals on the 6th day of Creation week about 6,000 years ago" (p. 1). This is the basis for the Creationists' theory. God, the designer of all, created life about 6,000 years ago versus 12-15 million years ago. These land animals mentioned would include the giraffe. Creationists also believe that creation and science are complementary ideas. This view is portrayed by Dr. John N. Moore (2008), a Professor Emeritus of Natural Sciences at Michigan State University, who says "…the science and research practices of both creationists and evolutionists involve the very same techniques, equipment, etc…. As a consequence, I avoid the expression "creation science." I prefer the use of a hyphen—i.e., "creation-science"; the hyphen conveys that two areas of human knowledge have been joined" (p. 1). Creationists trust that science and their beliefs are coherent. They use science, just like the Evolutionist, in order to support their theory. Creationists believe that the giraffe's neck was created by a designer with a specific purpose in mind. According to David Pittman (2011) who wrote the article "Walking Tall by Design," "… the idea that the neck became elongated stepwise over successive generations under environmental/selection pressures is now shown to be a great deal more complex than previously thought, with a whole assortment of structures and systems that need to be in place to accommodate the long neck….It illustrates the point that an organism is a finely balanced collection of interconnected (and often interdependent), systems. And the only One who can achieve such a delicate balancing act is the creative Genius who designed it in the first place" (p. 2). The Creationists believes the complex science behind the giraffe supports their theory which states that God created the giraffe on day six about 6,000 years ago. The giraffe appeared on this earth as one sees it today, and its long neck and legs remain unchanged, making the giraffe perfect for its environment. Unlike the Evolutionist's view that focuses more on the hypotheses rather than the evidence that supports them, the Creationist's does not require any additional hypothesis but focuses mostly on the research found. The scientific research supporting their theory revolves around the fossil record, the complexity and importance of co-dependent mechanisms in the giraffe, and the essential method of the birthing process.

The Rebuttal

The Fossil Record

The evidence found in the fossil record supports the theory which states: the giraffe's neck did not evolve but was created long, as one sees it today. Dr. Robert E. Simmons (2009), a behavioral ecologist specializing in the ecology of giraffes, believes in the Evolutionist view that the giraffe's neck evolved into a more complex and better-designed neck over time. In his scholarly article, he uses the fossil record to support his hypothesis. According to Simmons and Altwegg (2010) citing Mitchell and Skinner (2003), and Badlangana et al. (2009), "The earliest fossil ancestor of the giraffe…had skeletally short legs and neck, and occurred in India 12-15 million years ago. The giraffid [(an ancestor to the giraffe)], similar in size to the okapi showed long legs but an unelongated neck and arose about 12- 15 million years ago and went extinct about 9 million years ago. The medium sized *Paleotragus germaini* and the large *Samotherium* sp. exhibited elongated necks relative to their total vertebral column" (p. 9). Initially, this seems like logical evidence which supports the Evolutionists argument; however, there are a few problems that arise from this statement. The two fossils found exhibiting the giraffe could have very well been other cloven-hoofed animal species with short necks such as cattle or deer. In fact, Evolutionists claim the two fossils of the giraffe containing a short neck and short legs both lived on the earth at the same time (12-15 million years ago) as the giraffid with the long legs but unelongated neck. Because they existed simultaneously, one did not evolve into the other. This presents an obvious challenge to the Evolutionist's theory. The giraffid showing similar characteristics to the okapi very well could have been another animal or an okapi itself. There is no evidence it was an intermediate species. Evolutionist's lack the evidence to prove that the fossils they have found were in fact ancestors of the giraffe. The fossils discovered could have easily been any cloven-hoofed mammal, or even the fossil of a cow.

Another problem with the Evolutionists' view is the complete lack of intermediate fossils exhibiting the evolving giraffes that must have existed between the short-necked and long-necked giraffes. Even the Evolutionists believe the fossil recorded was too scattered to prove one hypothesis for their own theories. Simmons and Altwegg (2010) conclude: "At present, the fossil record is too patchy to support one hypothesis over the other" (p. 9). The problem with the "sex for necks" hypothesis is that the fossil record should show evidence of a gradually increasing neck length in males over time. The problem with the "competing browser" hypothesis is that the leg length should have increased simultaneously with the neck length, however, the fossil record has presented no evidence of this. There are no fossils displaying these "missing link" giraffes which make up the core foundation of this hypothesis. As Simmons and Altwegg (2010) citing Mitchell and Skinner (2003), and Badlangana et al. (2009) said, one fossil shows short legs and a short neck, and one fossil shows long legs and a long neck. Even the Evolutionists admit the fossil record is too scattered to prove the hypotheses. Creationist Dr. Carl Wieland, a surgeon and former atheist, is the founder of the Creation Science Association in Australia. According to Anderson and Wieland (2007), the fossil record shows no evidence of the short-necked giraffe. Short-necked quadruped (four-legged) fossils do, in fact, exist; however, these fossils resemble the Okapi which is a mammal with the same features as a giraffe except for a shorter neck. Anderson and Wieland (2007) claim, "When [they] see fossils of *Giraffa,* there are no short, intermediate and long-necked forms, let alone [ones] showing a progression" (p. 1). Based on the fossil record, the fossils of quadrupeds with short necks easily could have been okapis. More importantly, though, are the fossils not found. Archeologists and scientists have failed to find any fossils up to this point showing the giraffe with an intermediate long neck, and they certainly have not found numerous amounts of fossils which could be placed together to show the slow progression or the timeline of the neck evolution mentioned in these two hypotheses.

The Essential Mechanisms in Place as a Result of Hypertension

Another problem for the Evolutionists is that their theories do not consider the complexity and co-dependence of mechanisms that prevent hypertension as the neck elongates. According to research done by Mittchel and Skinner (2009) on the anatomy of the heart in giraffes, as the baby giraffe matures into an adult, its neck grows longer and its blood pressure increases. Zhang (2006) says, as a result of their long necks, giraffes have extremely high blood pressure and could potentially run into many problems if it were not for certain mechanisms they possess. This creates a problem for the evolutionist. According to Simmons and Altwegg (2010), "we need to determine what maintains giraffe's 2.5m above possible competitors when there are costs" (p. 10). These costs include predation rate, blood pressure and skeletal lengthening (Warren, 1974; Mitchell et al., 2006 as qtd in Simmons and Altwegg, 2010). As one can see, Evolutionists themselves recognize hypertension as detriment to their own hypotheses. As the neck and legs evolve, these mechanisms must simultaneously develop, perfect and complete, in order to keep the mammal alive. Graham Mitchell, is a zoologist at the University of Wyoming and believes in the Evolutionist's theory. In his scholarly article titled "An allometric analysis of the giraffe cardiovascular system," Mitchell (2009) says, "There has been co-evolution of a long neck and high blood pressure in giraffes. How the cardiovascular system has adapted to produce a high blood pressure… [is] largely unknown" (p. 1). An alarming problem in the Evolutionist's theory is admitted by this statement. The giraffe and its entire species would die if the mechanisms did not evolve in chorus. The Evolutionist agrees that the mechanisms would have had to evolve at the same time as the elongation of the neck, but they do not know how this would occur. The argument of complexity and compatibility is one that the Evolutionist has still to answer.

One of the mechanism the giraffe possesses is a thickening of the skin in order to keep it from excessive bleeding when injured (Mittchel & Skinner, 2010). Lynn Hofland has a B.S. in Environmental Engineering and is an Environmental Test Engineer at NASA Ames research center. He explains in his article, "Giraffes: Animals that Stand Out in a Crowd", how NASA has studied these unique mechanisms in giraffe legs in order to design a gravity suit worn by astronauts. According to Hofland (2013), "The secret lies in an extremely tough skin and inner fascia that prevents blood pooling [into the lower extremities]" (p. 2). The tough skin must be present because the neck of the giraffe is long. The Evolutionists must assume that, by chance, the skin thickened as the neck elongated, but they have no scientific evidence of this. The tough skin around the legs of the giraffe is one of the many mechanisms which would have had to evolve at the same time as its legs and neck in order to keep the species alive and reproducing.

Another mechanism found in the legs is the narrowing of the arterial walls (Ostergaard et al., 2011). Without the narrowing of the arterial lumen (interior of the artery) inside the leg, the blood would puddle in the hoof as a result of the high blood pressure. According to K.H. Ostergaard et al. (2011) who performed numerous dissections of the arterial artery, "…[the] narrowing at knee level is apparent in the newborn giraffe, not yet exposed to gravitational pressure" (p. 696). The dissection of the fetal giraffes proved that the giraffe is born with this trait already in place. The giraffe needs this mechanism as soon as it stands up because it is at that exact moment when the giraffe will experience high blood pressure due to gravity. This is a huge problem for the Evolutionists. If the mechanism gradually evolved with its neck over long periods of time, then the baby giraffes being born during this intermediate time period would not survive due to a non-functional arterial lumen.

Another mechanism the giraffe possesses is the jugular vein valves. According to Graham Mitchell's article, "The structure and function of giraffe jugular vein valves" published in 2009, "…the main function of the jugular vein valves is to prevent regurgitation of blood from the inferior vena cava and right atrium into the jugular vein and the number of valves [was concluded] to be fixed in utero" (p. 1). Without the presence of these valves, the blood would flow into the jugular vein, which is a vein that carries deoxygenated blood from the brain back to the heart, and cause the blood to re-enter the giraffe's head while it is lowered. This must be prevented. In order to keep the blood from flowing the opposite direction through the jugular vein and to maintain the cardiac output (the amount of blood pumped throughout the giraffe's body), the jugular valves must be fully functional (Mitchell, Van Sittert & Skinner, 2009). These jugular valves would have to evolve simultaneously with the long neck in order for the giraffe to live. According to Mitchell, Van Sitter & Skinner (2009), "… [the valves'] effectiveness in preventing regurgitation will depend on their capacity to withstand the hydrostatic pressure generated by venous return and the column of blood in the jugular veins…and position" (p. 179). In other words the valves must be strong and well-developed in order to withstand the pressure of the blood. If the valves are evolving over time in the neck as it elongates, then the valves which are only partially developed will not be strong enough to hold the blood and the giraffe would die. The effectiveness of the valves also depends on position (near or away from the heart). If the giraffe with the intermediate-length neck only developed the valves closer to the head instead of the valves closer to the heart, then the valves would not do their job, and the giraffe would die. The jugular valves are also seen in the giraffe during gestation. In dissections preformed on fetal giraffes, according to research done by Mitchell, Van Sittert & Skinner (2009), "the number of valves [per unit length] in each segment of the fetuses was the same as in adults, and so the number appears to be fixed in utero" (p. 180). The giraffe is born with this feature because, if absent, the baby giraffe would die at birth. The fact that the baby giraffe is born with this feature shows the importance of the feature for its survival. The giraffes that would have been born with only half-evolved systems would have died immediately after birth. The complexity and coherence of these mechanisms, which must be in place in order for the long-necked giraffe to live, point to a design that was present from the beginning of the giraffe's existence.

The Birthing Process of Giraffes

The last piece of evidence pointing to the Creationists view is the magnificent birthing process of the giraffe. According to Lynn Hofland (2013), "the birth of a new born giraffe seals the case for intelligent design" (p. 3). The birth process of the baby giraffe is indeed a remarkable process which again presents numerous problems for the Evolutionists' hypotheses. As researched by Hofland (2013), because the baby giraffe must face a drop of 1.5 meters from the mother, the exit through the birth canal must be perfectly designed in order for the calf to survive the fall. The female giraffe cannot squat during the birth nor lay down due to the threat of predators, so she must stand while giving birth (Hofland, 2013). The fact that the mother has to stand during the birth means the calf must immerge in a specific manner in order to withstand the fall. If the baby giraffe come out of the birth canal head first, the neck would break because of the weight of its body. In contrast, if the giraffe came out body first, "the neck would surely break as the body weight attempted to jerk the head out of the mother" (Hofland, 2013). According to Hofland (2013), "Such an apparent impasse is solved by the rear hips being smaller than the front shoulders, and the neck is just long enough to allow the head to pass through the birth canal [while] resting on the rear hips" (p. 3). If the baby giraffe did not have the right length neck to pass through the birth canal in this posture then the calf would fall and die. This creates yet another problem for the Evolutionist's theory. If the baby giraffes must have a certain structure in order to come out of the mother's birth canal, how did the giraffes with the intermediate-length neck survive? This question must be answered in order for the Evolutionist's theory to be proven correct. If they theorize that other systems of the mother evolved simultaneously to accommodate the birth of the intermediate species, they create a "domino effect." The female giraffe's birth canal would have to be perfect, so the calf with the longer neck could come out without breaking its neck. This is impossible in an evolutionary scenario. The female giraffe would not be able to change her birth canal before she birthed her calf. The calf's neck would come out first because the canal would be too short. The calf would fall to the ground and instantly break its neck. The birthing process is complex and depends fully on the flawless structure of the calf and mother. Evolution claims that the calf would change structurally over time, but this idea means the calf would die during birth. The birthing process of a giraffe directly supports the Creationist's theory. The giraffe was created with a long neck and was perfectly designed in structure to come out cleanly and survive the treacherous fall.

Conclusion

The birthing process as well as the fossil record and the essential mechanisms that counteract hypertension are the three specific reasons I believe the Creationists' theory. The giraffe was created originally with a long neck, long legs, and all the interconnect mechanism and processes showing incredible, intelligent design. The giraffe truly is an amazing creature with uniqueness and beauty recognized by all because of its height. The science behind the giraffe's structure is overwhelming, complex, and well-designed. Every mechanism inside the giraffe relies on the others in order to keep the towering beast standing. The sound, systematic science behind the design of this magnificent creature makes me love and appreciate them even more.

Works Cited

Anderson, Daniel, and Carl Wieland. "The giraffe's neck:Icon of evolution or icon of creation." *creation.com*. N.p., 5 Jan 2007. Web. 5 Nov 2013. <http://creation.com/the-giraffes-neck-icon-of-evolution-or-icon-of-creation>.

Hofland, L. (2013, November 5). *Giraffes:animals that stand out in a crowd*. Retrieved from http.//www.creationism.org/articles/giraffes.htm

Mitchell, G., & Skinner, J. D. (2009). An allometric analysis of the giraffe cardiovascular system. *Comparative Biochemistry & Physiology Part A: Molecular & Integrative Physiology,* 154(4), 523-529. Web.

Mitchell, E. (2013, July 13). *www.answersingenesis.org.* Retrieved from http://www.answersingenesis.org/articles/2013/07/13/bacteria-to-giraffes.

Mitchell, G., Van Sittert, S., & Skinner, J. (2009). The structure and function of giraffe jugular vein valves. *South African Journal of Wildlife Research*, 39(2), 175-180. Web.

Moore, J. (2008, January 24). *www.answersingenesis.org.* Retrieved from http://www.answersingenesis.org/articles/2008/01/24/attention-to-word-meaning.

Ostergaard, K., Bertelsen, M., Brondum, E., Aalkjaer, C., Hasenkam, J., Smerup, M., ... Baandrup, U. (2011). Pressure profile and morphology of the arteries along the giraffe. *Journal Of Comparative Physiology,* 181(5), 691-698. Web.

Pitman, D. (2011, October). Giraffes: Walking tall by design. Creation, 33(4), 28-31. Retrieved from http://creation.com/giraffe-neck-design.

Simmons, R. E., & Altwegg, R. (2010). Necks-for-sex or competing browsers? a critique of ideas on the evolution of giraffe. *Journal of Zoology,* 282(1), 6-12. Retrieved from http.//ehis.ebscohost.com.

Zhang, Q. (2006). Hypertension and counter-hypertension mechanisms in giraffes. *Cardiovascular & Hematological Disorders Drug Targets,* 6(1), 63-67. Web.

"Social Media in Nursing: Friend or Foe?"
by Leah Rachel Bode

Instructor's Notes

In this research paper students were to investigate how their future professions might be affected or influenced by social media or some other form of technology. Leah Rachel chose to argue that, though various forms of social media can be beneficial to nurses struggling to cope with the stress of their jobs, the potential professional risks far outweigh the personal benefits. Note how Leah Rachel's choice to open her essay with "the placenta incident" not only effectively captures the serious consequences suffered by many nurses who thoughtlessly upload work images to social media sites but also immediately orients readers to both sides of her argument. As you read the essay, locate sections of the argument which might be strengthened by additional examples or support.

Writers' Biography

Leah Rachel Bode will be a senior Nursing major at Cedarville University. After graduating, she hopes to pursue midwifery and one day serve God as a medical missionary. She loves the Lord, babies, friends and scrapbooking.

Social Media in Nursing: Friend or Foe?

When nursing student Doyle Byrnes uploaded a seemingly harmless image to her Facebook page, she never could have predicted the consequences that would result. The incident began when the eager student, during a class at Johnson County Community College, photographed herself leaning over a human placenta. Delighted with the educational opportunity before her, Byrnes smiled for the shot and then uploaded the image to her Facebook page. A flurry of activity resulted, and the college ultimately expelled the student for her unprofessional conduct and misuse of confidential information (Nursing Students). As "the placenta incident" illustrates, the presence of social media impacts the medical field extensively today, offering both promising benefits and devastating consequences. Social media carries the potential to effectively educate, unite, and enrich the medical community (White Paper 1). For example, websites such as Facebook offer nurses the ability to deepen connections with coworkers and process stress experienced at work, activities which can reduce emotional burnout. However, these benefits can also lead to harmful consequences when abused. Social media can improve the emotional health of nurses by fostering relationships among coworkers and encouraging meditative journaling; however, it largely erodes the security of the medical field because it incites nurses to violate patient confidentiality.

Social media significantly impacts the lives of millions, and before exploring this subject it is necessary to understand its definition and scope. Merriam-Webster's Online Dictionary defines social media as "forms of electronic communication... through which users create online communities to share information, ideas, personal messages, and other content." Variations of social media include blogs, podcasts, and sites such as YouTube, Twitter, MySpace, and Facebook (NSNA 1). Under the umbrella of social media, Facebook is one of the most popular websites, boasting of approximately 800 million users (McAndrew 2359). On any given day, approximately half of these individuals log in to their account to update information, peruse friends' pages and photographs, and chat with other users (2359). Social media saturates the lives of the world today; millions turn to it when communicating with friends, working, expressing emotions, keeping informed about current events, exercising, and traveling. As a result, lines are often blurred separating work, play, and time with friends. Like an oil spill, the use of social media is extremely challenging to control. Because it is convenient to use, versatile, and massively popular, it presents a formidable challenge for those attempting to regulate it. Consequently, members of the healthcare profession face great difficulty in addressing this problem, and the answers to this dilemma are far from black-and-white.

When used properly, social media provides desirable benefits to the medical community. Specifically, it can potentially promote emotional and mental health among nurses, a group of individuals who dealt with an enormous amount of stress on a daily basis. According to the National Institute for Occupational Safety and Health in the United States, nursing is "among the top 40 occupations with the highest prevalence of stress-related disorders" (Bourbonnais 20). Nurses often suffer from burnout, which is "emotional, mental, and physical exhaustion caused by excessive and prolonged stress" (Smith). In hospitals, emotional fatigue decreases quality of care and increases costs, which reduces the efficiency and competence of the nursing profession (Kowalski 1655). Alarmingly, approximately 15-45% of nurses in the western world suffer from emotional burnout (1654). When utilized appropriately, social media can potentially address and reduce the symptoms of exhaustion.

Social media can lessen the symptoms of emotional fatigue by improving relationships among nurses. A survey conducted by the Federal Ministry of Education and Research discovered that the level of emotional burnout experienced by a nurse depends in part on the quality of his or her interactions with others in the workplace (Kowalski 1660). The study noted that when nurses were dissatisfied by their relationships with other coworkers, they experienced higher levels of emotional exhaustion (1660). If relationships among nurses do in fact impact the prevalence of burnout, it is wise to improve these interactions in order to increase the quality of care and decrease costs. A study conducted in 2008 by the International Business Machines Cooperation displays how social media can improve relationships and foster fulfilling friendships in the medical community (DiMicco 711). For this experiment researchers created Beehive, a website designed to improve professional interactions. Analysts discovered that several employees used Beehive primarily to form relationships with coworkers they did not know. One participant in the study reported that Beehive "helps me connect to people personally…which makes me want to work with them" (716). Although this study focuses on one specific situation and environment, it displays how individuals can use social media to improve their professional relationships. Through websites such as Facebook, nurses learn about their coworkers' families, dreams, and activities, topics which can spark meaningful conversations in the workplace. Coworkers can also communicate with each other through private messages and in responses to informational updates. In doing so, nurses become involved in their coworkers' lives on a personal level, which can foster more enriching interactions while at work. If handled properly, social media sites can strengthen relationships between nurses, reducing the effects of emotional burnout.

Promoting internal health even further, social media can encourage nurses to meditatively journal in order to relieve stress and release tension. Oftentimes, nurses overlook their own needs in an effort to provide for others, which can dangerously affect their health (Charles 180). Karen Baikie, who is a clinical psychologist, writes that journaling can serve as an effective method of processing feelings experienced after a traumatic event (338). Blogs and other websites offer a place for nurses to express emotions, work through distressing situations, or therapeutically manage stress. Social media websites can provide a place for nurses to address their own needs and struggles, which can prevent "compassion fatigue" (Charles 180). Because journaling helps the left side of the brain balance out the emotions of the right side, it can boost the emotional health of nurses which will impact the efficiency and safety of the medical field (182).

Although social media appears to carry great potential for the nursing community, it is bereft with flaws, and the benefits quickly lose their value when examined closely. First, it is challenging to concretely prove that the benefits of social media outweigh the risks, for this subject is extremely speculative. Because of the complex nature of friendship, relationships, and the human mind, it is difficult to concretely prove the effectiveness of social media in promoting camaraderie and relieving stress. Additionally, these benefits are extremely subjective, depending on the personality, lifestyle, and choices of each individual. For example, one nurse may utilize her Facebook page in an entirely different manner than her coworker, yielding polar opposite results. Consequently, it is perplexing to predict consistent outcomes. Furthermore, there are other effective methods of addressing emotional burnout which usurp social media's role in nursing. For example, nurses can bypass social media altogether and adopt several other approaches when forming and maintaining relationships with coworkers. Lunch dates and coffee breaks are often more effective in strengthening friendships than private messaging over the web. Furthermore, the internet is not a necessary component in the journaling experience; individuals may find it more helpful to jot down meditations in a notebook or document on their laptop. Clearly, hospitals can address the issue of burnout without involving the presence of social media.

These benefits diminish even further in light of the devastating consequences that often result from the inappropriate use of these websites. In the past, nurses have breached patient privacy, violated the law, humiliated patients, and degraded the security and safety of the medical field while using social media. The root of the problem lies in the fact that the very nature of social media contradicts the essence of healthcare in the United States. Social websites focus "on communication, collaboration...connecting with people, and...sharing of ideas" (qtd. in Klitch-Heart 56). Blogs and sites such as Facebook "[encourage] openness, dialogue, and connection of ideas and people..." (57). However, this contradicts the foundational value of confidentiality which guides the nursing career. When members of the federal system created the Health Insurance Portability and Accountability Act (HIPAA) in 1996, they desired to "protect individually identifiable health information in all forms, both electronic and paper" (57). According to this policy, hospitals require medical staff to guard confidentiality diligently and prevent the disclosure of information that would easily identify their patients. However, nurses struggle to meet these requirements while exploring the candid and transparent world of social media.

Alarmingly, several myths cloud this topic and lead nurses astray, increasing further the dangers presented by social media. For example, troubles arise when nurses falsely believe that as long as they do not post their patients' names, the privacy of the individual is protected (NCSBN 3). On the contrary, however, "the definition of individually identifiable information includes any information that relates to the past, present or future physical or mental health of an individual" (NCSBN 1). Any piece of material that reveals the identity of an admitted individual is considered confidential; this includes room numbers and specific details regarding a patient's condition. When nurses misunderstand the definition of private information, problems result.

Additionally, threats emerge when nurses underestimate the size of the social media world, believing it to be confined to their circle of friends and thus easily controllable. On the contrary, however, social media stretches across the globe and provides easy access to countless pieces of information. Alarmingly, it is often impossible for a user to remove a piece of information from the internet once they entered it, for it takes only seconds for others to copy and paste the information (Anderson 39). Therefore, it is extremely easy for material only intended for specific audiences to spread. For example, in 2009 a group of nurses violated confidentiality laws after posting information about their patients on Facebook in order to prepare their coworkers for the next rotation. Although these women only intended to share information with the group, others were able to access the information, and the hospital reprimanded the nurses for their actions (Dimick).

These myths wield even more damage when coupled with the high prevalence of mobile phones, which accommodate nurses with easy access to social media. Approximately 350 million individuals access Facebook from their mobile devices, providing access to web pages in a matter of seconds (Boultin 8). Unfortunately, this does not allow much time for nurses to think through the consequences their actions may bring.

When nurses act according to these false beliefs, devastating consequences can result. In 2010, the NCSBN conducted a study which confirmed the abundance of social media-related offenses in the medical community. When NCSBN questioned forty-six boards of nursing about the occurace of offenses related to social media, thirty-six claimed they "had received complaints about nurses who had violated patients' privacy by using social networking sites" (Hillman 48). In one example, a nursing student received harsh punishment after handling social media improperly. While on her pediatrics rotation, she snapped a photo of her young patient who was battling leukemia. Including his room number in the image, she posted the picture to her Facebook page. Consequently, the school expelled the student for the way she violated HIPAA and placed the hospital in jeopardy (NCSBN 5). A second example involved a nurse in Wyoming who posted a picture of a patient's x-ray to her Facebook page. Amused at the foreign object stuck in the man's rectum, the nurse acted immaturely and unprofessionally and compromised the security of the hospital (Freeman 49).

In the United States today, social media heavily impacts the realm of healthcare. When used appropriately, it can promote emotional health among nurses who experience a high rate of emotional burnout. In order to maintain holistic health, nurses must discover ways to reduce stress and process complex emotions. Positive interactions among coworkers can effectively address symptoms of burnout. Additionally, nurses can journal online in order to meet personal needs and untangle their thoughts. Although social media can provide tools to improve health, these benefits are speculative and difficult to prove. Unfortunately, they dwindle further in light of the immense consequences that social media can spawn. In recent years, its presence has degraded the competence and security of the medical field, causing confidential and private information concerning patients to leak out. Problems arise when nurses believe the myths surrounding social media and lack wisdom and discernment in posting information. The presence of mobile devices complicates this problem, as access to social media is always at a nurse's fingertips. Nurses sometimes violate HIPAA laws through the use of sites such as Facebook, leading to a loss in jobs, violations of the law, and even imprisonment. Clearly, the risks presented by social media erode the security of the medical field and negate the benefits.

When nurses breach confidentiality, they commit a serious offense against the patient and the hospital in which they work. This is unacceptable in the medical field; not only does it violate defy the law, but it disrespects the patient whose trust has been violated. Serving and caring in hospitals all over the country, nurses owe a great deal of respect for the patients under their management, simply because the man or woman bears the image of God and carry great worth in his sight. Expected to care for men and women of all ages with compassion and competence, nurses must continuously strive to provide the privacy their patients deserve. Mother Teresa elegantly encapsulated the essence of nursing when she stated, "It is not how much you do but how much love you put in the doing" (Mother Teresa). Protecting patient confidentiality essentially displays the respect that a nurse holds for her patient. It is a shame that many view the interactions on Facebook as more important than the patient lying in the next room. Nurses should never sacrifice the protection of a patient for a cheap laugh but instead find constructive methods of dealing with stress. In the medical field, nurses must strive to honor and protect those in their care, understanding the responsibility they bear to the patient, their family, the hospital and ultimately to God.

Works Cited

Baikie, Karen and Kay Wilhelm. "Emotional and physical health benefits of expressive writing." *Apt.rcpsych.org*. The Royal College of Psychiatrists, 2012. Web. 1 Dec. 2012.

Bourbonnais, Renee, Monique Comeau, Michel Vezina, and Guylaine Dion. "Job Strain, Psychological Distress, and Burnout in Nurses." *American Journal of Industrial Medicine* 34 (1998): 20-28. Web. Nov. 2012.

Boulton, Clint. "Facebook Needs Phone to Battle Google for Mobile Ads." *eWeek* 28.20 (2011): 7-8. *Academic Search Complete*. Web. Nov. 2012

Charles, Jennell P. "Journaling: Creating Space for "I". *Creative Nursing* 16.4 (2010): 180-184. *Academic Search Complete*. Web. 11 Nov. 2012.

DiMicco, Joan, David Millen, Werner Geyer, Casey Dugan, Beth Brownholtz, Michael Muller. "Motivations for Social Networking at Work." *Umsl.edu*. IBM Research, 2012. Web. Nov. 2012.

Dimick, Chris. "Private Policies for Social Media." *Journal of AHIMA*. American Health Information Management Association, 16 Jan. 2010. Web. 25 Oct. 2012.

Freeman, Greg. "Facebook firings show privacy concerns with social networking sites." *Healthcare Risk Management*. 31.5 (2009): 49-52. *CINAHL Plus*. Web. 6 Dec. 2012.

Klitch-Heartt, Eira I and Susan Prion. "Social Networking and HIPAA: Ethical Concerns for Nurses." *Nurse Leader* 8.2 (2010): 56-58. *Academic Search Complete*. Web. Nov. 2012.

Kowalski, Christoph, Oliver Ommen, Elke Driller, Nocole Ernstmann, Markus AWirtz, Thorsten Kohler, and Holger Pfaff. "Burnout in nurses—the relationship between social capital in hospitals and emotional exhaustion." *Journal of Clinical Nursing*. 21.9 (2012): 1490-1491. *Academic Search Complete*. Web. 18 Nov. 2012.

McAndrew, Francis T., and Hye Sun Heong. "Who does what on Facebook? Age, sex, and relationship status as predictors of Facebook use." *Computers in Human Behavior* 28.6 (2012): 2359-2365. *Academic Search Complete*. Web. 17 Nov. 2012.

"Mother Teresa." *Doonething.org.* The Emily Fund. Web. 7 Dec. 2012.

"Nursing Students Kicked out for Placenta Photos." *Cbsnews.com.* The Associated Press, 3 Jan. 2011. Web. Nov. 2012.

"Recommendations For: Social Media Usage and Maintaining Privacy, Confidentiality and Professionalism." *Nsna.org.* National Student Nurses' Association, Inc. Web. Nov. 2012.

Sauter, Steven, Lawrence Murphy, and Joseph Hurrell. "Prevention of Work-Related Psychological Disorders." *American Psychologist* 45.10 (1990): 1146-1158. *PsycARTICLES.* Web. Nov. 2012.

Smith, Melinda, Jeanne Segal, and Robert Segal. "Preventing Burnout." *Helpguide.org.* Helpguide, July 2012. Web. 29 Nov. 2012.

"White Paper: A Nurse's Guide to the Use of Social Media." *NCSBC.com.* National Council of State Boards of Nursing, 2011. Web. Nov. 2012.

"America's Responsibility in a War Not Our Own" by Rebecca Ehnert

Instructor's Notes

In this persuasive essay, Rebecca sets up a duel argument: the US was partially responsible for the plight of the Mayan people in Guatemala, and, thus, is responsible to provide aid. Notice how she supports and refers to those arguments throughout the essay, never losing sight of her purpose in writing. Using references to her thesis like, "obligation to help," "should provide continued assistance," and "must take responsibility," to support the first half of her argument and "America's obsession with ending communism," "the American-backed army targeted the indigenous people," and "partially responsible for the economic hardships" to support the second half of her argument, Rebecca supports her thesis well.

Writers' Biography

Rebecca Ehnert is studying Spanish at Cedarville with a psychology minor and is in the honors program. She enjoys academic writing including research papers. She likes to travel and hopes to work in a cross-cultural ministry setting.

America's Responsibility in a War Not Our Own

I walk down the main street in the center of the small Guatemalan town, smiling at passersby as I go along. I come to a woman dressed in a colorfully decorated traditional outfit and look directly at her. Her unique outfit, short-stature, and dark skin are clear signs that she has mostly indigenous Mayan ancestry. Although I smile, she quickly turns her face and looks the other way. I cannot figure out why she, like the other Mayan people I have come across, is timid – almost fearful. Only later do I realize how strongly the society of Guatemala affects the mindsets of these indigenous people. The Mayan people of Guatemala are social outcasts, nearly invisible. This has been especially true since the recent civil war in which the army specifically targeted the Mayan people. This civil war has drastically shaped their country, but here in America many people know little to nothing about this life-changing war. When asked why she believed the war in Guatemala has not gotten as much attention as other wars in Central America, Rigoberta Menchú (an indigenous woman) replies, "One of the reasons is racism itself. We [the indigenous people] don't have means of communication in our hands. The media and politics has never allowed our people to speak through them" (McPherson 173). These people suffered great losses during the war, yet they have a minuscule voice when it comes to getting their story told. The whispered memories of this war, which exist primarily in the stories of those who lived through it, have been intentionally hushed by the powerful fabricators who began it all over five decades ago. This "silent war" warrants not only recognition but action as well. The United States should aid the Mayan people of indigenous descent in Guatemala because they continue to suffer long-term effects such as poverty and poor education from the recent civil war, which the United States was partially responsible for starting and continuing as they funded the Guatemalan government.

The responsibility to help the Mayan people began when the United States was involved in starting the recent civil war in Guatemala, which led to the murders and suffering of countless Mayan people. It was a natural response for America to become involved because Guatemala appeared to be in need of assistance. The United States assumes responsibility for maintaining liberty throughout the world as America is the land of the free and the home of the brave. When a situation, which compromises the freedom of a group of people, arises, the United States is usually the first country to step in, show its bravery, and try to fix the problem. During the time of America's fight against communism, "Central America's ruling classes learned that merely by labeling their opposition as 'Bolshevik' or 'Communist' they could usually win US support, ranging from direct armed intervention to economic and military aid" (Booth 26). In the 1950s, President Árbenez and his government at the time began to implement a "Law of Agrarian Reform" which would redistribute land and give more to the poor in an effort to "overcome the economic backwardness' of the country and 'improve the quality of life of the great masses'" (Wilkinson 83). The opposition of President Árbenez began to scheme how to stop this plan, which would take land away from the large United Fruit Company. They accused the government which "might best be described as a liberal reform movement" of having communist tendencies; therefore, America got involved (*Latin America: Its Problems and its Promise* 251). With help from the CIA, the opposition overthrew Árbenez, so the country needed a new president. The United States tried to control the election outcomes in order to determine the type of government in Guatemala. American representatives helped initiate a "republic based on a constitutional democracy" ("Guatemala Information"). Shortly after the war, this government failed in many democratic ways such as not allowing the vast population of illiterate people to vote. The people do not have all the freedoms contained in what Americans view as a true democracy. America's obsession with forming a democracy in Guatemala was one large factor in starting the civil war. If the Guatemalan army did not have the support from America, the war may have never started. The original opposition of Árbenez asked the CIA to help because they knew the task would be too difficult for them to accomplish on their own. Had the war never started, the Mayan people would not have suffered. The United States government provided aid at the start of the war that began the brutal conflict lasting 36 years, so they have the responsibility to continue to provide assistance in Guatemala until the damage from the war is reversed.

Not only did they help start the war, but also the United States aided the Guatemalan armed forces throughout the recent civil war. The United States was involved in many external wars, and according to historical authors and professors of political science, Booth, Wade, and Walker, "This outside manipulation of Central American politics... intensified and prolonged their conflicts" (Booth 2). This was definitely true in Guatemala where the United States government was economically involved throughout the war. America provided funding for the official Guatemalan military to fight the so-called communists: "From 1946 through 1992 the United States provided US$1.8 billion in military assistance to the region [of Latin America] 98 percent of it to Guatemala" (Booth 26). Without this funding, the Guatemalan army would not have had the resources that it used during the war. This is more money (in current US dollars) than the United States spent on the American Revolution, the War of 1812, the Mexican War, and Spanish

American war combined (Daggett 1). There can be no honest claim that the United States was not significantly involved in the economic aspect of the Guatemalan civil war. This type of claim implies that four wars in America's history were insignificant based on the amount of funds used during wartime. This funding provided by the United States prolonged the conflict in Guatemala also prolonging the suffering of the Mayan people. The US was partially responsible for the continual suffering of the Mayan people, so they should help correct these wrongs.

Although the United States government was involved in Guatemalan politics during the war, many believe it holds little responsibility because the Guatemalan military personnel were the ones actively involved during the killings of the war; nevertheless, the United States was involved in the war even from a distance. Even if the Guatemalan army is mostly responsible for the atrocities of the war, this does not let the United States go free of all responsibility. One side cannot assume all responsibility. There is combined fault in many situations from the war. The American CIA and other government groups were supporting the Guatemalan government throughout parts of the war both politically and economically. As the Guatemalan government performed countless murders and injuries against the Mayan people, the United States provided aid; therefore, the United States holds responsibility for these actions as well.

The Guatemalan army, which received aid from the United States throughout the civil war, targeted the Mayan people. During the Guatemalan civil war "the crisis was particularly cultural and racial," and the Guatemalan government fixated on "the poor ... indigenous groups who spoke little Spanish and had been banished to isolated mountain villages" (McPherson 82). The government targeted the Mayans directly, but the indigenous people also suffered from unintentional factors. During the civil war "most of the violence and massacres took place in the predominantly indigenous areas" (Booth 155). The indigenous people living in the mountains suffered a majority of the damages partly because of the geographical positions of the war. Today, "more than half of Guatemalans are descendants of indigenous Mayans and a substantial proportion of the population are of mixed European and indigenous ancestry" (Chamarbagwala 43). Most Guatemalans identify themselves as having some indigenous ancestry. The majority of people in Guatemala can identify with those targeted during the civil war. Since so many people suffer, the United States must take responsibility for their actions.

As the American-backed army targeted the indigenous people, many Mayans were killed in Guatemala during the civil war. Historians consider the civil war a "'dirty war'... in which thousands of people [were] murdered or simply 'disappeared'" (Wiarda and Kline 89). Many of the people who "disappeared" were taken to remote parts of the country to be killed. The families of these lost people never knew where their loved ones were. For many years, the families of those victimized during the war never received any form of apology or explanation. As early as in the first years of the war, "in the cities and countryside suspects of left-wing sympathies picked up by the army increasingly tended to either turn up dead or remain 'disappeared.' The army and police consistently denied responsibility" (McClintock 83). Although thousands of people suffered and died during the war, the Guatemalans responsible for the murders never admitted to the atrocities. This caused emotional distress to family members from the mystery of where their loved ones could be. As a majority "more than four-fifths of the deaths from the civil war era were indigenous" (Booth 155). The families of these people suffered from the loss of loved ones and from the anxiety of the unknown details of their loved ones' last days. Because of their anti-government opinions, some families also had legitimate fear of retaliation. The Mayan people suffered numerable losses and emotional distress; the United States should provide retribution to the families who lost loved ones.

Aside from those who suffered physical and emotional damage, other indigenous people who were living in the highlands were displaced during the civil war. Many indigenous people left their homes as the militants took over the land that once belonged to them because "much of the violence... took place in Guatemala's indigenous highlands or lowland jungles and away from urban areas" (Booth 139). The poorest people living in the mountains of Guatemala owned precious highlands, which the army used for strategic positioning. The Guatemalan government easily took advantage of the poor, and "most of the poor were indigenous groups who spoke little Spanish" (McPherson 82). The army confiscated land that indigenous families had passed down for generations. Without this land, the Mayan people had no choice but to re-locate to areas without jobs. They continue to suffer from this displacement, which occurred during the war, so the United States must provide permanent housing and other forms of humanitarian aid for these people.

Although the Mayan indigenous people of Guatemala were poor before the war, they suffer increased poverty because of displacement during the civil war. In 1987, in the middle of the war, the percent of population living on $2 per day or less was highest in recorded history at over 70 percent of the total population ("Data: Guatemala"). This percent of severely impoverished people in Guatemala has slowly decreased since the end of the war but continues to be one of the highest in the world. Per capita GDP (Gross Domestic Product), signifying the average standard of living in the country, increased during the civil war; "however, Guatemalan economic growth did not increase the income of the poor" (Booth 139). Although the country got richer, the poor stayed poor. The distribution of wealth in Guatemala meant that the richest people in Guatemala gained wealth without sharing any of it with the poorest people groups. Records show that "between 1970 and 1984 income distribution concentrated increasingly in the hands of the wealthiest fifth of the people," still the Mayans did not benefit because "the income share of Guatemala's poorest fifth shrank" in that same amount of time (Booth 139). The indigenous people were extremely poor before the beginning of the war, and this level of poverty has only worsened. The increased wealth of the country of Guatemala as a whole has not improved the lives of the poor, indigenous people. Although the country grows richer, the people who suffered during the war do not see any of this wealth; therefore, their lives continue to be difficult in post-war Guatemala. The Mayan people are in need of economic help after the war. America helped create a war, which left thousands of people in need of economic assistance. Because the United States is partially responsible for the economic hardships faced by the Mayan people, the U.S. should provide aid.

The indigenous people of Guatemala continue to have poor education, resulting from the displacement and poverty caused by the war. The Mayan indigenous people continue to be the poorest people group in Guatemala today. In 1995 as well as in 2008, the indigenous people of Guatemala "were significantly poorer and less educated" than the people with European ancestry (Booth 155). In Guatemala, public education is theoretically free, but the fees associated with sending a child to school are so high that many poor parents choose feeding their family over educating their children. Another factor leading to an uneducated generation of indigenous people is that "poor access to schools in rural communities and a significant deficit of bilingual instructors posed serious impediments to indigenous education" (Booth 155). The schools that indigenous children attend are not up to normal standards. The displacement of families during the war resulted in an increased number of extremely poor indigenous people. These people often have no way to pay for the expensive school fees. Even if there were a way to send their children to school, the types of schools present in the areas that the indigenous people live in are not up to the standards necessary to provide the students with successful and prosperous adult lives in Guatemala. The war was the cause of an entire generation being under-educated, and the cycle continues; therefore, America has the responsibility to provide financial and other forms of aid to educate these people.

Although the Guatemalan government has provided some retribution for these hurting Mayans who lost family members or houses and continues to provide aid to the indigenous people, it is not enough. The Guatemalan government needs help because "it is increasingly difficult these days for isthmian governments [those of Central American countries] to reduce poverty" (Booth 9). There are myriad of problems which factor into the poverty crisis of Guatemala. The small and shaky government of Guatemala is having a hard time providing for its poorest people in this complex situation. Outside organizations like the Hispanic Clarification Commission knows that the indigenous people need help. The HCC "viewed the treatment of Guatemala's Mayan people as so central to the problem of returning Guatemala to peace that it encouraged the government" to focus on training and preparing the Mayan people for public societal life "and to provide reparations for the injuries done during the violence" (Booth 155). The indigenous people continue to suffer many consequences of the war. Outside groups have noticed a need for aid and retribution to the victims of the civil war. The internal Guatemalan government is unable to provide all the assistance needed. An outside source must step in, or these indigenous people will continue to suffer in Guatemala. The United States has the responsibility to step in, not only as the traditional humanitarians of the world, but also as offenders of the civil war.

Change for these indigenous people is possible. Experts consider the negative changes seen in Latin America in recent decades to be "limited, incomplete and perhaps even reversible" (Wiarda and Kline 611). Latin America in general seems to be doing well. In the last few decades "Latin America has gone from 70 percent rural to 70 percent urban, and from 70 percent illiterate to 70 percent literate" (Wiarda and Kline 611). These changes are averages across Latin America. Each country in Central America has its differences, but all five have similar histories and cultures. Perhaps Guatemala could mirror the improvements seen in other Latin American countries in recent decades. The indigenous Mayan people may be the last to see these improvements, but it is not out of the question to see significant change for the Mayan people in the next few decades.

The United States should aid the Mayan people of Guatemala who continue to suffer from the recent civil war that the United States was partially responsible for starting and continuing as the Guatemalan government targeted and murdered indigenous people and forced them out of their homes, which led to increased poverty and decreased education of the indigenous people. The Mayans have not received sufficient assistance in order for their lives to go back to normal. It has been difficult for the indigenous people to assimilate into the society. Although it has been difficult, the Mayan people have not given up. One victim of a violent attack during the war says, "Even though you never forget, you have to live always with the memory, but we have come together as a community" (Wilkinson 213). The people are not sitting there feeling bad for themselves, not doing anything to improve their lives. They are building their towns back and re-claiming their lives. The Mayan people are doing the best they can but cannot undo everything that the war has done on their own. The United States could provide a stipend for each family that suffers from the war. If it is too difficult to identify the families that are suffering, the American government could pay a sum of money to the country of Guatemala to provide social services such as welfare for the suffering people. If finding the correct place to allocate money remains too difficult, the United States could designate a representative to investigate needs in Guatemala. This representative could find the hurting people, especially Mayans who go unnoticed. The United States could then be confident that the money would go towards helping people who truly need it. There are many ways that the United States could repay the Guatemalan people who suffered because of the actions of America during the civil war. Providing any retribution would be better than doing nothing, so America should begin reparations now.

Works Cited

Booth, John A., Christine J. Wade, and Thomas W. Walker. *Understanding Central America: Global Forces, Rebellion, and Change.* Boulder: Westview, 2010. Print.

Chamarbagwala, Rubiana and Hilcías E. Morán. "The Human Capital Consequences of Civil War: Evidence from Guatemala." *Journal of Development Economics, Business Source Complete.* Web. 20 Sept. 2013.

Daggett, Stephen. "Cost of Major U.S. Wars." *Federation of American Scientists.* Congressional Research Service. Web. 29 June, 2010. 2 November 2013.

"Data: Guatemala." *The World Bank.* The World Bank. Web. 2 Nov. 2013.

"Guatemala Information" *Import Export Business & International Trade Leads - FITA Global Trade Leads.* The Federation of International Trade Associations. Web. 2 Oct. 2013.

Latin America: Its Problems and its Promise. Ed. Jan Knippers Black. Boulder: Westview, 2011. Print.

McPherson, Alan L. *Intimate Ties, Bitter Struggles: The United States and Latin America since 1945.* Washington, D.C.: Potomac, 2006. Print.

McClintock, Michael. *The American Connection: State Terror and Popular Resistance in Guatemala.* Volume 2. London: Zed, 1985. Print.

Wiarda, Howard J., and Harvey F. Kline. *Latin American Politics and Development.* 7th Edition. Boulder: Westview, 2011. Print.

Wilkinson, Daniel. *Silence on the Mountain: Stories of Terror, Betrayal, and Forgetting in Guatemala*. Boston: Houghton, 2002. Print.

"Benefits of Philosophical Diversity in Art" by Raymond Cordova

Instructor's Notes

Raymond writes a persuasive paper arguing that Christians can benefit intellectually from non-Christian art. I had tasked him with taking a definitive stance on a controversy relating to Christianity and the arts. Observe how Raymond thoroughly develops each paragraph, supporting his claims with multiple examples. He is still working out his style in this paper (it's a bit wordy at points), but Raymond's triumph in the paper is his determination to understand viewpoints that differ from his own. Bravo, Raymond.

Writers' Biography

Raymond Cordova is an English major from Boca Raton, Florida. Raymond's interests include reading and writing about intellectual, scientific, and theological history. He enjoys taking long walks and watching foreign films with his wife.

Benefits of Philosophical Diversity in Art

As Robert Hugh Benson explained in *Papers of a Pariah*, "Ignorance may be bliss, but it certainly is not freedom…The more true information we can acquire, the better for our enfranchisement" (34). A scholarly approach to the arts should embody this mindset in order to produce intellectual and spiritual maturity. On the other hand, intellectual impairment is the inevitable result of the mind's prohibition from anything not explicitly Christian. The scholar should not limit intellectual curiosity for the sake of keeping his beliefs untainted; this is not only an immature lack of discernment, but also a gross mishandling of man's God-given reason. Contrarily, intellectual curiosity should be encouraged and praised for its inclusive relationship with knowledge. One must discern and dissect differing philosophies for a comprehensive knowledge of the world. The most effective methods of expressing one's worldview are through artistic mediums; in artwork, the artist's philosophical convictions and underlying emotions are carefully embedded for the scholar to uncover. Valuable perspective and understanding are gained by interpreting art from differing worldviews. Artistic expression enlivens emotion and human nature, allowing the scholar to explore and unearth these concepts in depth. The Christian scholar's knowledge and comprehension of the world deepens after studying and experiencing art from differing worldviews.

One artistic work that enhances the intellectual's understanding of humanity is The Scream, by Edvard Munch. *The Scream* expresses the feelings of anxiety, loneliness, and illness better than any other modern work of art. Munch stated his goal with *The Scream* was, "the study of the soul, that is to say the study of my own self." Munch was in turmoil throughout his life and, while a priest's son, was not a self-confessed Christian. When analyzing *The Scream*, valuable perspective can be gained concerning human emotions and outlooks on life. The depicted figure's facial expressions convey a deep sense of abandonment, and its sexless nature shows a brokenness and emasculation. Contributing to the sense of loneliness, two figures walk away from the main character. Also, the twisted appearance of the backdrop conveys a confusion and spiraling disorder that inhabits the surrounding world. Munch explained this feeling: "I sensed a scream passing through nature; it seemed to me that I heard the scream. I painted this picture, painted the clouds as actual blood. The color shrieked. This became The Scream." Valuable content regarding the human condition is present in this artistic work for the Christian to observe, discern, and consider in light of the Holy Scriptures.

Leland Ryken, in *The Liberated Imagination*, rejects the truthfulness of secular works: "No matter how great an artist's technique may be, or how sensitive the portrayal of human experience is, a work of art is finally false if it limits reality to the temporal, physical world or omits God's existence from its picture of reality." Yet, truth is found in accurate portrayals of humanity. Absence of the supernatural does not lessen the realities of sorrow or distress. To adequately answer the world's problems, one must firstly be well-acquainted with them. The dire need for rescue from the world's flaws cannot be fully realized unless one carefully and unbiasedly discerns them. The fallen nature of creation, humanity's depravity, and the degenerative cycle of post-fall nature, directly coincide with Biblical revelation. By temporarily viewing the world from a non-Christian perspective, one gains a more comprehensive understanding of humanity and the disastrous effects of sin on creation. The figure's face shown in *The Scream,* exudes a common feeling within the lost soul—alienation. This alienation and loneliness results from the absence of fellowship with God. It conveys the loneliness of the unsaved life, and the confusion that results from recognizing something is amiss within oneself. The twisting nature of the backdrop shows the chaos and disorder occupying the enclosing world. This "scream" described by Munch is echoed within the scriptures, such as in Romans 8:22: "We know that the whole creation has been groaning as in the pains of childbirth right up to the present time." The verse speaks about the secular recognition that the Earth is in a sinful bondage and groans in pain. The Christian mind can use this perspective to achieve greater understanding regarding the depravity of life and find common ground with those who do not hold to Christian theology. *The Scream* is an example of non-Christian expression that adequately communicates several aspects of the issues facing humanity. For these reasons, *The Scream* is beneficial for the Christian to examine for greater knowledge and intellectual maturity.

Another example that shows artwork from different worldviews being profitable for the Christian observer is *The Persistence of Memory.* Created by Salvador Dali in 1931, *The Persistence of Memory* is a forefront example of modern surrealist art. Surrealism aims to combine dreams and reality into artwork; it stems from Dadaism, a style deeply mingled in the political far-left. Not only was Dali an artist, but also a philosopher who studied the works of Freud and Nietzsche. Dali's *The Persistence of Memory* provides insight into his philosophical worldview. The painting is a compilation of many concepts including time, death, reality, and life. Three melting clocks are depicted in the painting which convey a seemingly snail-paced passing of time and the finiteness that limits everything in its grasp. One clock lays still solid, but covered by ants, suggesting the gradual decay and anxiety associated with time. There lies an undefined figure in the middle of the painting which likely symbolizes the artist himself. The figure resembles a fish abandoned, suffocated, and dead on dry ground without breath. Upon examination, *The Persistence of Memory* conveys a confusion and merge of the dream world and reality. This painting struggles to understand time's decaying effects and the perpetual disintegration of all matter. When seen in the light of Christian theology, one can understand time is not limitless, but created with fixed boundaries by the boundless God (Ps. 90:4). The reason time injures all matter is due to the consequences of sin upon this world; all matter is now subject to decay and death following the Curse. For the secular mind, the idea of time and perpetual decay can be numbing and cause the confusion exhibited in Dali's painting. For the Christian mind, however, this painting presents an in depth look at a common view held by secularists concerning time. It also gives the Christian a new perspective on time and the finiteness of creation. The objection regularly raised asserts paintings such as this espouse surrealistic philosophy and purposefully confuse the recipient(s); because of this intentional misleading, it is not worthy for study. However, as one can see, there is much content relevant to humanity within the painting, and the work can help one better understand the unbeliever's mind in regards to time and death. *The Persistence of Memory* is worthy artwork for the educated Christian to benefit from by studying the ideas and conflicts within the work.

Christians must begin tearing down the walls that inhibit curious and reflective thought. Whether it be surrealism, Dadaism, or nihilism, there exist remnants of truth and perspectives that are valuable to the Christian walk. In order to effectively communicate the nature of humanity and the nature of this universe, one must be open to all ideas and philosophies regarding them. To be intellectually closed off to specific artwork from differing philosophies hinders the mind from a more complete comprehension of humanity. The Christian should not be afraid to dissect artistic work from differing worldviews, but should embrace this diversity of content, in the goal of furthering knowledge and understanding.

The Scream by Edvard Munch

The Persistence of Memory by Salvador Dali

Works Cited

Benson, Robert Hugh. Books for Libraries Press, 1967. Print.

Faerna, José María (1995.) New York: Harry N. Abrams. p. 16.

"Quick Facts." Becoming Edvard Munch. The Art Institute of
    Chicago. 6 May 2012.

Ryken, Leland. The Christian Imagination. Eugene, Oregon: WIPF
    and STOCK Pub, 2005. Print

"The Mammal with Heart" 3rd
by Hannah Gaitan

Instructor's Notes

All well-written texts incorporate appeals to pathos (emotions) as well as logos (logic). In this award winning essay, Hannah Gaitan effectively incorporates both into what could have been a solely logos driven, and thus, uninteresting, topic. After all, what is emotional about the circulatory system of a giraffe? Hannah shows her readers. Can you identify specific examples of pathos in this essay? How about specific examples of logos? Hannah also chose to include visuals in her essay. Why do you think she did so? What role do the visuals play? When might you choose to include visuals in a text of your own?

Writers' Biography

Hannah Gaitan is a second-year Pre-veterinary Medicine major from Boulder, Colorado. Hannah enjoys scientific writing, specifically dealing with animals, but finds creative writing and poetry to be difficult. She spends most of her time, however, studying for her classes and gaining hands on experience in the field of veterinary medicine. Her hobbies include equestrian sports, running, and hiking. She also enjoys hanging out with her family, boyfriend, and black lab, Buddy.

The Mammal with Heart

The scene is an exotic African safari. The sun begins to set as excited tourists look out over the savannah. While looking out into the distance, the tourists spot a majestic giraffe leaning down to drink peacefully from a calm body of water. Then, to the surprise of all, as the magnificent creature raises its head from the water, it faints and collapses to the ground. This would be quite a sight! Of course, if one has ever seen a giraffe at the zoo or on a safari, he would notice that the giraffe does not, in fact, collapse dramatically onto the ground after it raises its head from drinking. However, fainting is one of the many problems that could inhibit a giraffe if it did not possess the unique and perfectly designed circulatory system that it does. The giraffe towers over all the other mammals on earth. An average adult male can reach a height of eighteen feet; ten feet from the hoof to the shoulder and an additional eight feet coming from the length of the neck alone (Pitman, 2011). Due to the giraffe's extreme anatomical structure, its circulatory system must be uniquely designed. This essay explains the need for hypertension (high blood pressure) in the giraffe, the structure and size of the heart in the giraffe, and four unique mechanisms, located throughout the circulatory system, which prevent problems that occur as a result of hypertension.

The giraffe (*Giraffa Camelopardalis*) is the tallest mammal on earth. Since the giraffe's head ranges anywhere from eight to ten feet above its heart, its heart must pump extremely hard to supply the brain with the oxygen and nutrients it requires (Zhang, 2006). Therefore, compared to humans, giraffes have exceptionally high blood pressures (Zhang, 2006). The high blood pressure is referred to as hypertension. The average blood pressure is also commonly called arterial pressure. According to Ostergaard et al. (2011), giraffes have a mean arterial pressure (MAP) of 350 mmHg from the hoof to the brain and 250 mmHg from the heart to the brain. This is extremely high compared to the human MAP, which is roughly 100 mmHg. However, the "arterial pressure at the entrance to the skull is surprisingly similar to that of other mammals, including humans (approximately 100mmHg)" (Ostergaard et al., 2011, p. 691; Brondum, 2009; Hargens et al., 1987). The pressure of the blood entering into the brain is extremely low compared to the pressure it takes to send the blood from the hoof to the brain or from the heart to the brain. However, according to Zhang (2006), "The blood pressure would need to be higher than 205.6 mmHg for blood not only to reach the brain, but also to be able to perfuse the vascular bed and maintain normal function of the brain" (p. 64). Because of its remarkable height, the giraffe's heart must be strong enough to pump the blood a great distance in order to reach the brain at the proper pressure and supply it with oxygen and nutrients.

One may naturally assume that the giraffe's heart must be disproportionally large in order to overcome the force of gravity and carry the blood to the brain. However, that is not the case. It was experimentally determined by Mitchell and Skinner (2009) that the giraffe's heart mass depends on the size of the giraffe. They dissected fifty-six giraffe hearts, weighed them, and compared the weight to the mass of the giraffe. They concluded that the heart's size is proportional to the weight of the giraffe. In the ten giraffe fetuses that they dissected, they found that the heart was larger than the body mass, but this is usually the case among all mammals (Mitchell & Skinner, 2009; Holt et al, 1968). Since the size of the giraffe's heart is not surprisingly big in proportion to its body, how does it supply the brain with the oxygen- and nutrient-rich blood it needs?

In order for the heart to pump the blood up the carotid artery to the brain, the heart must be strong enough and be able to overcome the hydrostatic, or pressure due to gravity (Zhang, 2006). However, the size of the heart does not determine its strength. Instead, it is the structure of the heart that determines its strength (Mitchell & Skinner, 2009). According to Mitchell and Skinner (2009), they found, experimentally, that the structure of the heart is determined by the neck length. The further the brain is away from the heart, the higher the blood pressure, thus the magnitude of hypertension in giraffes is dependent on the neck length (Mitchell & Skinner, 2009). The high blood pressure affects the thickness of the walls of the left ventricle of the heart. (Mitchell & Skinner, 2009). Therefore, the longer the neck, the more hypertrophy, or thickening, occurs in the left ventricle. The left ventricle is the lower left chamber in the heart that pumps blood to the entire body. Without the thickening and strengthening of this ventricle, the heart would not be able to pump a sufficient amount of blood to the brain or body of the giraffe (Mitchel & Skinner, 2009). The hypertrophy of this ventricle occurs because the ventricle must work exceptionally hard in order to pump the blood up the carotid artery to the brain of the giraffe. As the giraffe grows, the neck becomes longer and hypertrophy of the left ventricle increases. The graph below demonstrates this relationship between the neck length and the left ventricle wall thickness, where "LVWT" represents the left ventricle and the "IVWT" stands for interventricular wall thickness which is irrelevant to this study.

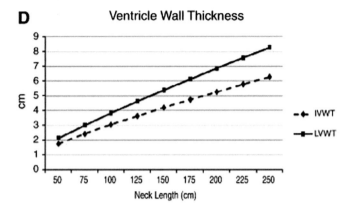

D   **Ventricle Wall Thickness**

(Mitchel, Skinner, 2009, p. 526)
Hypertrophy of the left ventricle increases until full maturity is reached (Mitchel & Skinner, 2009). This was proven true by Mitchel and Skinner (2009) as they dissected the hearts and found that giraffes with longer necks possessed a left ventricle that was thicker. The picture below shows a cross section of a fetal giraffe's left ventricle, interventricular wall, and right ventricle (heart A) compared to the mature adults' (heart B). While looking at this picture, one will notice the increased hypertrophy in the left ventricle (labeled "LV") in the adult heart (B) compared to the fetal heart (A).

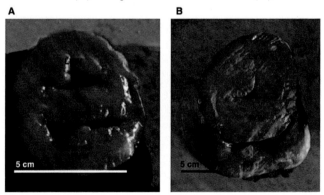

(Mitchel & Skinner, 2009, p.527)
According to Mitchel and Skinner (2009), "[Left ventricles] are massively hypertrophied in giraffes, a process [their] data show

is gradual and starts after birth" (p. 526). After the giraffe is born, it experiences a continual growth in blood pressure as its neck becomes longer. Without the increase of hypertrophy of the left ventricle as the giraffe develops, it would not survive because its heart would not be strong enough to pump the blood to the brain. Although the giraffe's heart is not surprisingly big for its body, the heart is extremely strong and is able to pump the blood to the brain.

The hypertension the giraffe needs to supply blood to the brain has the potential to cause multiple problems within the giraffe, however, there are four specific mechanisms that have been designed into its system that prevent these problems. The first of the four mechanisms are the jugular valves. The jugular vein is a large vein that returns blood to the heart from the head. When a giraffe lowers its head to take a drink of water, there is a possibility that blood could enter the jugular vein from the heart because of the high blood pressure. This must be prevented in order to keep the blood from flowing the opposite direction through the jugular vein and to maintain the cardiac output (the amount of blood pumped throughout the giraffe's body) (Mitchell, Van Sittert & Skinner, 2009). Based on an experiment done by Mitchell, Van Sittert, and Skinner (2009), the jugular valves' main function was indeed concluded "to direct the large amounts of blood, returning to the heart via the interior vena cava, into the right atrium, and to prevent its flow into the jugular vein" (p. 180). They also concluded that these valves develop during gestation. Giraffes have two jugular veins, right and left (Mitchell, Van Sittert & Skinner, 2009). During this experiment the jugular veins were opened and the number of valves and the position of valves were determined (Mitchell, Van Sittert & Skinner, 2009). It was discovered that the number of valves was of no significance. A long jugular vein could sometimes possess the same number of valves as a short vein (Mitchell, Van Sittert & Skinner, 2009). However, the position of the valves was found to be significant (Mitchell, Van Sittert & Skinner, 2009). According to Mitchell, Van Sittert, and Skinner (2009), while dissecting the jugular veins of twenty five adult giraffes and five fetal giraffes, they found a higher percentage of valves were located at the proximal end, close to the heart, than at the distal end, further from the heart. Four of the giraffes did not contain any valves at the distal segment of the jugular vein. According to Mitchell, Van Sittert, and Skinner

(2009), the fact that the jugular valves were found closer to the heart indicated that their primary function was to prevent "regurgitation of interior vena cava and right atrial blood into the jugular vein when the giraffe is in the head down position" (p. 179). As the giraffe lowers its head the valves close, and as the giraffe raises its head, returning to its original position, the valves reopen (Mitchell, Van Sittert & Skinner, 2009). The jugular valves, when closed, must withstand the hydrostatic pressure of the blood in the jugular vein and the pressure of venous blood that has already returned to the heart in order to be effective (Mitchell, Van Sittert & Skinner, 2009). The jugular valves do not develop with growth, but are in place during gestation. According to Mitchell, Van Sitter, and Skinner (2009), while dissecting the fetal giraffes, jugular valves were found to be present during gestation. This means that the valves do not develop as the neck elongates but are established before birth (Mitchell, Van Sittert & Skinner, 2009). If jugular valves were not present near the heart, then upon lowering the head blood from the heart would flow back into the jugular vein. Consequently, too much blood would flow back into the brain and not enough blood would remain in the heart to maintain a sufficient cardiac output.

The second mechanism that the giraffe possesses is a unique feature in its leg similar to the G-suit that fighter pilots wear. A G-suit is a specially designed suit that is worn by fighter pilots that places pressure on the legs and lower abdomen in order to keep the blood from pooling into their lower extremities when they begin to experience extreme forces. Giraffes have a built in "G-suit" that prevents leakages, due to hypertension, from capillaries in the giraffe's legs (Khfahl, 1992). Based on an experiment performed by Ostergaard et al. (2011), the pressure exerted on the legs increases closer to the hoof. This is true because of the force of gravity. The maximum arterial pressure that was measured was 350mmHg (Ostergaard et al., 2011). Since there is an increase in pressure, the arterial lumen (the inside of the artery) knee adjusts by gradually narrowing toward the hoof (Ostergaard et al., 2011). The gradual narrowing of the arterial lumen happens two to four centimeters below the knee (Ostergaard et al., 2011). The picture below shows the site where the tissue can be located, and also displays the tissue which was surgically removed and stained to clearly show the sudden narrowing that occurs in the arterial lumen about two to four centimeters below the knee.

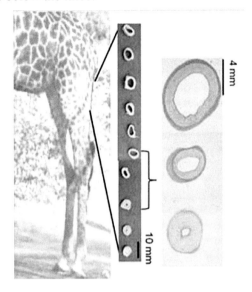

(Ostergaard et al., 2011, p. 693)
This is the G-suit-like structure that giraffes contain in order to withstand the effects of hypertension. As found by dissecting the tibial arteries, Ostergaard et al. (2011) determined that the narrowing of the arterial lumen was found in the fetal giraffe as well. Indicating the giraffe is born with this feature, from the moment they stand up, they are able to adapt to the high blood pressure. The skin of the giraffe also thickens at the legs, preventing the capillaries from rupturing into the leg (Mitchel & Skinner, 2009). Without the drastic morphology of the arteries in the legs of giraffes and the increase in the thickness of the skin, the arterial pressure would be too great due to gravity, and the capillaries would burst causing blood to puddle in the hoofs (Ostergaard et al., 2011).

The third and fourth mechanisms that the giraffe possesses, in order to adjust to high blood pressure, are the *rete mirabile* and a special, complex series of mechanisms that restore the blood in the brain after the head is lifted (Pittman, 2011). These two mechanisms prevent the opposing problems of too much blood flow to the head and too little blood flow to the head. As the giraffe bends its long neck down to get a drink of water, the amount of blood flow to the

129

brain would cause the blood vessels in the brain and eyes to rupture if it were not for the *rete mirabile* or "marvelous net" (Pittman, 2011). According to Pittman (2011), "When the head is lowered, special shunts in the arteries supplying the head restrict blood flow to the brain, diverting it into a web of vessels" (p. 2). The marvelous net is a series of small blood vessels which form a web-like structure (Pittman, 2011). When the giraffe lowers its head to drink, the arteries direct the blood into special vessels which are elastic and keep the brain protected from an overflow of blood. The network of vessels near the base of the brain expands and allows the blood to enter the brain at a normal (100mmHg) arterial pressure (Pittman, 2011). The next mechanism is a "unique anastomosis [or connection] between the carotid and vertebral arteries" (Goetz, 1995; Lawrence, 1948 as qtd in Mitchell, Skinner, 2009, p. 523). This connection prevents fainting when a giraffe lifts its head (Mitchell, Skinner, 2009; Goetz, 1995; Lawrence, 1948). Mitchell and Skinner (2009) refer to Goetz (1957) by saying, "[the connection] directs carotid artery blood into the cerebral perfusion, and an increase in cerebral perfusion pressure [then results]" (p. 523). As the giraffe lifts its head, blood from the heart travels up the carotid artery which is connected to the blood vessels in the brain. The connection between the arteries then directs the blood to the cerebral perfusion, which is a series of blood vessels in the brain. The pressure of these vessels (cerebral perfusion pressure) then increases, and the blood is quickly restored to the brain (Mitchell & Skinner, 2009). Without the *rete marible,* as the giraffe lowers its head, the blood vessels in the head and eyes would burst. Similarly, without the special connection between the carotid and vertebral arteries the giraffe would lift its head up and then faint, due to lack of blood flow to the brain.

The circulatory system of the giraffe is a truly complex system which demands high blood pressure to provide the brain with a sufficient amount of blood, a specifically structured heart that has enough power to produce this pressure, and four mechanisms that allow the giraffe to function despite its high blood pressure. Now, imagine again, the group of tourists on the exotic African safari. They spot a giraffe lowering its head to get a drink of water. Now, when the giraffe raises its head from the drinking, one can appreciate the complexity of the circulatory system and all of the steps it must successfully accomplish in order to keep a graceful, towering creature from collapsing.

Works Cited

Kofahl, R. (1992, March). Do drinking giraffes have headaches?. *Creation*, 14(2), 22-23. Retrieved from http://creation. com/do-drinking-giraffes-have-headaches

The article "Do drinking giraffes have headaches?" written by Robert E. Kofahl, Ph.D. summarizes the unique features that the giraffe's body contains in order to cope with its high blood pressure. The author discusses the powerful heart of the giraffe and the features that allow the giraffe to bend over and take a drink without the heart pumping too much blood into the brain. Kofahl then discusses the importance of the giraffe spreading its legs and lowering its heart to drink water. He then explains the importance of the jugular valves located in the neck that open and close to allow and prevent blood flow. In this article he discusses the spongy tissue that is located under the brain that controls the blood flow to the brain. Then Kofahl discusses the importance of the counter-pressure mechanisms that prevent leakage of blood from the capillaries. The perfectly designed features that allow the giraffe to bend its head to drink water are presented clearly and simply in this article. I will be able to use this article to give an overall summary of the circulatory system of the giraffe and be able to explain its important adaption that takes place when the giraffe lowers its head to drink.

Mitchell, G., & Skinner, J. D. (2009). An allometric analysis of the giraffe cardiovascular system. *Comparative Biochemistry & Physiology Part A: Molecular & I ntegrative Physiology,* 154(4), 523-529.

This scholarly article was written by G. Mitchel and J.D. Skinner who work at the Centre for Veterinarian Wildlife Studies in South America and The Department of Zoology and Physiology at the University of Wyoming. The authors present data found by their calculations in the form of charts and graphs that compare the blood pressure and wall thickness of the ventricles to the mass and length of the giraffe's body and neck. The data was retrieved from previously derived allometric equations. They also discuss three hypothesis for why giraffes have high blood pressure. Mitchel and Skinner give explanations and average quantitative data of the cardiac hypertrophy, stroke volume, heart rate, and cardiac output that occurs in adult giraffes. This is invaluable information about the overall cardiovascular system in giraffes. This accurate, well written, scientific article will help me explain the anatomy of the circulatory system in giraffes and how the circulatory system functions uniquely with the giraffe's long neck.

Mitchell, G., Van Sittert, S., & Skinner, J. (2009). The structure and function of giraffe jugular vein valves. *South African Journal of Wildlife Research,* 39(2), 175-180.

This article was written by Graham Mitchel, Sybrand J. Van Sittert, and John D. Skinner. The authors are either faculty on the veterinarian staff or work in the Zoology and Physiology Department of the University of Wyoming or the University of Pretoria. This article discusses the anatomy of the jugular vein in the giraffe. They conducted an experiment which consisted of the dissection of the jugular veins of twenty five juvenile to adult giraffes and five fetal giraffes. Mitchel, Van Sittert, and Skinner discuss the results and come to a conclusion about the importance of location and anatomy of the valves located in the jugular vein in giraffes. The authors discuss the problem of blood re-entering the cranial veins and how it is prevented. They explain the anatomy of the uniquely designed jugular vein and valve placement that make the giraffe able to bend without blood regurgitating into the brain. This well-developed experiment and accurate, scholarly information will be helpful in explaining the anatomy of the valve system and its important role in the giraffe's circulatory system.

Ostergaard, K., Bertelsen, M., Brondum, E., Aalkjaer, C., Hasenkam, J., Smerup, M., ... Baandrup, U. (2011). Pressure profile and morphology of the arteries along the giraffe. *Journal Of Comparative Physiology,* 181(5), 691-698.

This Scholarly article was written by Ostergaard K. et al. The authors measured the arterial and venous pressure in the foreleg of the giraffe. They also measured the area of the arterial lumen in the hind leg and found that it was suddenly narrowed below the knee of the giraffe. The tissue was collected from ten euthanized giraffes and the pressure was measured from four giraffes under local anesthesia. The data was expressed in the form of pictures and graphs that displayed the pressure related to the distance from the hoof. Ostergaard KH et al discussed the morphology they found in the arteries from the knee down. They also explained the importance of high blood pressure in giraffes and the morphology that takes place in the arteries below the knee due to the hypertension in the giraffe. The authors also measured the elastin in the arteries and provided the data in the form of a chart that related the volume fraction of elastin with the distance from the heart. This well conducted, well explained, and accurate experiment will help me explain the unique built in "G-suit" with which the giraffe is born and the importance of the morphology in the arteries to adjust to the high blood pressure.

Pitman, D. (2011, October). Giraffes: Walking tall by design. *Creation,* 33(4), 28-31. Retrieved from http://creation.com/giraffe-neck-design

The article "Walking Tall...by Design" was written by David Pitman and appeared in the magazine Creation on October 2011. Pitman summarizes the anatomical features that make the giraffe unique compared to other mammals. He discusses the circulatory system and the design it has to prevent the giraffe from fainting when raising its head. In particular, he discusses the jugular valve system and the spongy membrane that is located below the brain. Pitman concludes this section by discussing the rapid response of these mechanisms that enable the giraffe to quickly raise its head when danger is evident. He also explains the thickness in the giraffe's leg skin that prevents the giraffe from losing too much blood when it is injured. This article is short and clearly highlights the special features of the circulatory system of a giraffe. I will be able to use this article to give a brief overview of the anatomy and functions of the giraffe's circulatory system and how the system prevents certain expected problems.

Zhang, Q. (2006). Hypertension and counter-hypertension mechanisms in giraffes. *Cardiovascular & Hematological Disorders Drug Targets*, 6(1), 63-67.

This article, written by Qiong Gus Zhang, discusses the high blood pressure in giraffes and how the organs within the giraffe adapt to the hypertension. He uses former research and mathematical equations to prove that giraffes do indeed have a higher blood pressure than humans. He then calculates average blood pressure in giraffes. Zhang also explains that giraffes must have a higher blood pressure in order to supply the brain with oxygen and nutrients due to their exceptionally long necks. The author discusses the negative side effects of hypertension that result in humans and then explains how the giraffe's body counteracts these. He specifically discusses the hypertrophy, or thickening, of the heart and in particular the left ventricle, and the kidney's normal function despite its location near the heart. This article was printed in a scientific journal, and the author Qiong Gus Zhang works at the California Institute of Technology. I found this article to be very helpful because it gave a good summary of other previously discovered data. This article will be used to help me explain the importance of hypertension in giraffes and how the organs are designed to handle

"Monkey Business" by Kaleen Carter

Instructor's Notes

Writing an expository essay on a controversial topic can be difficult because the genre requires complete neutrality and a commitment to unbiased reporting. What are some strategies Kaleen Carter uses in this essay to effectively achieve this goal. What is the scope of her topic? How do you know? Is it important for an author to articulate the scope of his or her topic? Why or why not?

Writers' Biography

Kaleen Carter is a second-year AYA Life Science Education major from Colorado. She loves sharing her knowledge and helping others when she can. She enjoys being around people and spends most of her time with others. This summer, she is marrying an officer in the United States Air Force and moving to Oklahoma where she will continue her education.

Monkey Business

The alarm going off early in the morning, the coffee, the commute to work, and the job were familiar to John Scopes as he started his next year of teaching biology. Though many parts of his schedule remained unchanged, Scopes altered his curriculum in a way his school opposed. Scopes chose to teach the theory of evolution to his high school classroom, violating the school's rules. This decision landed him in court in what would become known as the Scopes "Monkey Trial." Though this trial did not come to a clear cut verdict on evolution's place in education, the case immensely impacted the science classroom throughout the United States, bringing the quiet disagreements on the origin of the earth, circulating the education realm since Darwin's publication of *Origin of the Species* in 1859, into a loud public debate that has found its way into courtrooms (Armenta & Lane, 2010, p. 76-77).

Both evolution and intelligent design advocates present reasons on why their viewpoint should be taught. Evolutionists believe students must have an evolutionary background in order to fully appreciate and understand science. Without this teaching, schools limit their students' potential through intentionally avoiding this important topic. Eugene C. Scott quotes Theodosius Dobzhansky saying, "Without…[the light of evolution, biology] becomes a pile of sundry facts some of them interesting or curious but making no meaningful picture as a whole" (2008). This side, also, accuses its opponent of an ignorance regarding intelligent design, which prevents most educators from teaching the subject in an appropriate and academic manner (Discovery Institute, 2013).

On the other hand, intelligent design advocates believe the teaching of only evolution limits students' intelligence, while adding intelligent design to the curriculum improves critical thinking along with science education (Ratvitch, 2012, p. 199). Some claim the teaching of their theory should be allowed for the sake of "fairness" and "academic freedom" (Ravitch, 2012, p. 192). Other supporters of this recent theory call out for "fairness" in a different manner. These individuals desire the elimination of evolution form the classroom due to its relation to a religion, secular humanism. They see this as a fair response to court decisions, which have pushed intelligent design out of the classroom based on its religious background and parallels. If their theory cannot be taught in school because of its religious tendencies, then evolution should be banned on the same terms (Scott, 2008).

This seemingly unsolvable debate has become a problem for science educators. For many teachers, this debate has resulted in reassignments, loss of jobs, and lawsuits, as with John Scopes. Most do not understand what they can or cannot say, leading to avoidable legal action. Despite the confusion, teachers can gather several guidelines for teaching the origins of the earth from the mass of court cases involving the two prominent theories (Stader, Graca, & Stevens, 2010, p. 73). This essay discusses the guidelines for teaching the origins of the earth as determined in several court case rulings.

Before looking at court cases and rulings, an understanding of the relationship between creationism and intelligent design, the Frist Amendment, the Establishment Clause, and the definition of science is necessary. Though intelligent design does not mention God but an intelligent designer, it was ruled as an equivalent to creation science in *Freiler v. Tangipahoa Parish Board of Education* (1999), which the court in *McLean v. Arkansas Board of Education* (1982) ruled as a religious theory based on its literal interpretation of the Genesis creation account (Moore, Jensen, & Hatch, 2003, p. 769-770). In accordance with The First Amendment and the Establishment clause, the church and state must remain separate. Furthermore, all government institutions, such as schools, must remain religiously neutral. They cannot participate in any teaching or activity that promotes or inhibits a religion, thus, when religion is taught, it must be done in an objective manner and in appropriate classes (Scott, 2008). Science has been defined as an explanation of "natural phenomena by reference to natural processes." All scientific theories must be observable and lead to predictions. Scientists should be able to prove any theory or prediction true or false through observable material or events, and they should be able to retest theories. Additionally, science does not involve any supernatural events under any circumstances (Lofaso, 2009).

The four items previously mentioned play largely in court decisions regarding the place of these two theories in the classroom. The first big case after the Scopes Trial, *Epperson v. Arkansas* (1968), took place in Arkansas in response to anti-evolution laws (Armenta & Lane, 2010, p. 77). A public school banned the teaching of evolution and the use of textbooks supporting this theory. The US Supreme court found the statute existed to prevent teaching contradictory to the Genesis account of creation. As a result, the court ruled such a statute violates the constitution because the statute promotes a religion and adjusts the curriculum to better suit those practicing the religion (Moore, Jensen, & Hatch, 2003, p. 767).

Because states could no longer ban the teaching of evolution, they started making statutes requiring "equal time" or "balanced treatment" for creationism. These statutes, also, found themselves in court. Judge William R. Overton in *Mclean v. Arkansas Board of Education* and Justice William Brennan in *Edwards v. Aguillard* judged these statutes as a violation of the First Amendment. Overton found this law promoted a certain religion, namely Christianity. Brennan went further in applying the "Lemon Test" developed in *Lemon v. Kirtzman* 1971. This test has three parts. Each proposed law cannot fail any of the three sections in order to be considered constitutional. "Any government action must (1) have a secular purpose, (2) have a primary purpose that neither advances nor inhibits religion, and (3) not foster an excessive government entanglement with religion." Brennan found the requirement of equal treatment between these two theories fails every section of the Lemon Test, making this decision highly unconstitutional (Armenta & Lace, 2010, p. 77).

Courts prioritize the constitutionality of schools higher than the appeasement of the majority, thus the rulings in these cases override student or community protest toward the teaching of evolution or advocacy for intelligent design. The interpretation of the Establishment Clause of the First Amendment, which states the United States cannot pronounce a national religion, has caused governments to focus on religious toleration versus pleasing the majority. Regardless of popular vote, schools must remain religiously neutral. Courts do not consider this an infringement on an individual's freedom of religion because evolution is religiously neutral and "the free exercise of religion is not accompanied by a right to remain insulated from scientific findings incompatible with one's religious beliefs" (Moore, Jensen, & Hatch, 2003, p. 768-769).

As a result, teachers cannot refuse to teach evolution or use their freedom of speech to teach intelligent design regardless of their own personal beliefs or the beliefs of others. In John E. Peloza v. Capistrano Unified School District, the court decided a school could either reassign or dismiss a teacher who refuses to teach evolution. Because evolution is not a religion, the teaching of such material does not infringe on a teacher's freedom of religion. In *Webster v. New Lenox School District #122* (1990), the court stated that the changing of curriculum by a teacher to include intelligent design advocates religion. Because teachers are governmental employees, their freedom of speech becomes limited, as their speech reflects back onto the institution. Thus, the First Amendment does not give teachers the right to teach intelligent design, and, when they do, they defy constitutional values (Moore, Jensen & Hatch, 2003, p. 768-770).

For a similar reason, the government can finance the purchase of evolutionary textbooks but not textbooks supporting intelligent design. In *Willoughby v. Stever*, William Willoughby protested the use of tax payers' money to fund "secular humanism" through the support of the theory of evolution. To Willoughby's dismay, the court ruled such funding to be completely constitutional because evolution fits the definition of science, not religion. Additionally, the courts found governmental funding of intelligent design as religious affiliation. Although the government cannot fund textbooks that support this theory, they can purchase textbooks that call intelligent design unscientific (Moore, Jensen, & Hatch, 2003, p. 768).

The courts agree with such textbooks in that intelligent design is not science. In *McLean v Arkansas Board of Education*, Federal Judge William Overton spoke against intelligent design for its lack of scientific value, which weakens its educational value. Overton states "A theory that is by its own terms dogmatic, absolutist, and never subject to revision is not a scientific theory." This perspective founds its facts on the Bible verses re-testable information and relies heavily on the supernatural, making it fall short of the definition of science (Moore, Jensen, & Hatch, 2003, p. 769). If it were to be considered science, this term would need to be redefined, but for now, this theory has no place except to be taught objectively in appropriate classes such as a comparative religion class (Ravitch, 2012, p. 196).

Many states have recognized intelligent design does not belong in the scientific classroom due to its foundation on religion and lack of educational merit. Consequentially, some school districts have required teachers to read a disclaimer or have stuck one on the evolutionary textbooks. Though this seems harmless, most disclaimers have lost in court because they have religious purposes. In 1999 and 2005, *Freiler v. Tangipahoa Parish Board of Education* and *Kitzmiller v. Dover Area School District*, both convened to settle disputes regarding disclaimers. In *Freiler v. Tangipahoa Parish Board of Education,* the court ruled against the disclaimer due to its religious purpose observed in the line, "the scientific theory of evolution…should be presented to inform students of the scientific concept and not intended to influence or dissuade the Biblical version of Creation." This school tailored the disclaimer to fit the educational needs of a specific religious group, which promotes religion. The court in *Kitzmiller v. Dover Area School District* declared the disclaimer in Pennsylvania violated the constitution. Judge Jones saw the disclaimer directed students toward a religious alternative and religious outside resources; discriminated against evolution, causing students to question the theory without critically thinking or finding scientific evidence to support their thoughts; and perverted evolution's place in the scientific community. In Georgia, *Selman v. Cobb Country School District* resulted due to a sticker placed on textbooks referring to evolution as "a theory, not a fact." The court deemed the sticker unconstitutional because only the religious consider evolution a theory while those in the scientific realm consider it a fact. By calling evolution a theory, the school sided with the religious side of the debate and promoted religion (Armenta & Lane, 2010, p. 78-79).

Some schools have decided to discuss the flaws of evolution to help resolve disputes with intelligent design advocates in the community. Discovery Institute supports this teaching. In fact, they press for evolutionary textbooks to offer full coverage of evolution including its strengths and weaknesses. Furthermore, they encourage "critical scrutiny" of the theory. Currently, three states have laws protecting teachers when they teach this material, and seven states require the teaching of scientific flaws or controversies; however, teachers must teach such flaws with a secular intent. If teachers have a purely secular intent, they are allowed to discuss other theories involving the origins of the earth as determined in *Edwards v. Aguillard* (Discovery Institute, 2013).

Even after a plethora of court cases, the debate on the validity of evolution and intelligent design continues. Though disagreements and heated conversations still take place, teachers can feel secure when teaching the origins of the earth by understanding the court cases and the courts' decisions. Courts have decided teachers must work to keep schools religiously neutral and material in appropriate classes. They require schools to prioritize student achievement and learning above the advancement of religion. Through these mandates, courts hope to help bring evolution and intelligent design into their appropriate places in the scientific classroom.

References

Armenta, T. & Lane, E. K. (2010). Tennessee to texas: Tracing the evolution controversy in public education. *The Clearing House*. 83(3), 76-79.

Discovery Institute. (2013, Feb 11). Discovery's science education policy. 27 Feb. 2014.

Lofaso, M. A. (2009). Curriculum Issues. *Religion in the public schools: A road map for avoiding lawsuits and respecting parents' legal rights.* ,Washington, DC: Americans United for Separation of Church and State. 67-69. 27 Feb. 2014.

Moore, R., Jensen, N., & Hatch, J. (2003). Twenty questions: What have the courts said about the teaching of evolution and creationism in public schools?. *BioScience.* 53(8), 766-771.

Ravitch, S. F. (2012). Law, religion, and science—Determining the role religion plays in shaping scientific inquiry in constitutional democracies—The case of intelligent design. *Contemporary Readings in Law and Social Justice.* 4(1), 191-204. 27

Scott, C. E. (2008). Cans and can't of teaching evolution. *National Center for Science Education.* 27 Feb. 2014

Stader, L. D., Graca, J. T., & Stevens, W. D. (2010). Teachers and the law: Evolving legal issue. *Clearing House.* 83(3), 73-73.

"Sleep and Its Effects on the Human Body" by Meredith Merritt

Instructor's Notes

One of the most difficult aspects of expository writing is deciding what details to include and which to eliminate. Providing too much detail can bog down the flow of an essay, while too little can render the essay vague and unclear. In her essay on sleep, Meredith Merritt provides an appropriate amount of detail. What are some strategies you use for deciding what to include and what not to include in your essays? What are some ways to organize an essay around the details?

Writers' Biography

Meredith Merritt is a sophomore Allied Health major from Pennsylvania. She is currently preparing to enter the field of occupational therapy in the hopes of putting to good use her love for people. She enjoys a wide range of hobbies, from reading literature to carving down mountains on her snowboard. Her heart, however, remains firmly attached to working at summer church camps.

Sleep and Its Effects on the Human Body

The hour hand rests on the ten, the minute hand on the twelve. Five more minutes, then the lights go out and life once more reaches a momentary pause. Diligence or not, the drooping eyes and the groggy mind indicate the growing call for sleep and mark the arrival of the end to yet another day. While this occurrence remains an integral part of daily life, what happens during this period of rest remains somewhat of a mystery to many. In *Sleep: The Mysteries, the Problems, and the Solutions*, Carlos Schenck, an associate professor at the University of Minnesota Medical School, deepens this marvel: "Considering that people on average will spend 25 years of their lives asleep, it's surprising how little most of us know about what goes on when the lights go off" (1). Many people may reflect upon this "wonder" in feeling a sense of laziness from spending such a significant portion of their lives unconscious and completely inactive. Modern discoveries concerning sleep, however, reveal that this perspective—viewing sleep as an expression of laziness—rings hollow with falsehood. The fact that humans sleep remains undeniable, but scientists continue to broaden their understanding in discovering the true details of this process. With this continually growing breadth of knowledge, scientists can now make claims as to the importance of the processes that take place during such activity and how they play into the differentiation between adequate and inadequate amounts of sleep.

In the early 1900s, the invention of a new technology, the electroencephalogram (EEG), led to a scientific breakthrough. The initial use of an EEG involved placing electrodes externally on the patient to monitor electrical impulses within his or her body. Shortly thereafter, scientists discovered certain reactions taking place within the brain that produced an electrical current similar to those studied throughout the body (Epstein and Mardon 11-12). This finding allowed for utilization of such tests in studying the brain.

Subsequently, in 1929, Hans Berger, "known as the father of EEG," used this technique to document the first ever recordings of human sleep (Pressman and Orr 12). In more recent studies, researchers utilize "a standard sleep recording, called a *polysomnogram,* [which] is a continuous, all-night tracing of electroencephalographic (brain-wave), electrooculographic (eye movement), and submental electromyographic (chin muscle) events" (Pressman and Orr 14). In others words, these studies involve analysis of more than simply brain waves – they also monitor patterns of eye movement as well as the electrical activity within the facial muscles. Scientists then compare such measurements to that recorded during the waking hours. According to *A Good Night's Sleep* by Lawrence Epstein, M.D., and his coauthor, Steven Mardon, "The brain was not passively and uniformly shutting down during sleep but rather passing through several different patterns of activity in an orderly fashion" (12-13). This confirmation of brain activity revolutionized the study of sleep.

Following the discovery of sleep's systematic nature, scientists categorized it into five major steps known as the sleep cycle. The main qualitative division they found led to the classification of the first four stages as non-REM (rapid eye movement) sleep, and the fifth stage as REM, or dream sleep. Within each progression through this pattern, various factors mark the transition from one stage to the next. Stages one and two, for instance, represent the initial, shallow levels of sleep; stages three and four enter a much deeper level; and REM involves the intermittent, shallow, and highly active levels.

In more detail, the first stage one enters involves a period of light sleep from which he or she awakens easily. During this approximately five-minute stage, EEG studies revealed changes in the brain waves as they transitioned from alpha waves to theta waves (Epstein and Mardon 13-14). The units for such measurements are cycles per second. This designation refers to the frequency with which waves in the EEG recordings appear. Smaller waves of greater frequency and smaller amplitude (height) represent higher levels of brain activity, whereas larger waves of lower frequency and larger amplitude reveal lower levels of brain activity. In the case of specific wave types, the alpha wave pattern includes 8-12 cycles per second, while the theta wave pattern includes 4-7 cycles per second (Epstein and Mardon 13-14). Therefore, during this first stage of sleep, the transition from alpha waves to theta waves shows the decline in brain activity.

The second stage of sleep, a type of transition stage, occurs periodically throughout the night in approximately ten to twenty-five minute intervals (Epstein and Mardon 15). People typically spend about half of the night in this stage as they enter and re-enter it multiple times in between other stages. Further testing reveals that this phase involves still eyes, a slower heart and breathing rate, and sporadic brain activity (Epstein and Mardon 15). As Epstein explains it, this sporadic brain activity presents itself through multiple sets of a "brief [burst] of fast activity called sleep spindles . . . [and] a K-complex, which scientists think represents a sort of built-in vigilance system that keeps you posed to be awakened if necessary" (15). The discovery of these types of brain activity further emphasizes the level to which sleep is truly an active process.

The next two stages fall under the category of deep sleep. As the name implies, stages three and four involve a deeper level in which much of the restorative properties come into effect. For the average sleeper, the sum of these thirty-minute segments typically constitutes about twenty percent of a single night of sleep (Epstein and Mardon 16). During this time, the brain waves transition again, this time from theta waves to delta waves (Epstein and Mardon 15). Delta waves are even larger, slower brain waves. Their rate usually ranges from 0.1 to 3.5 cycles per second (Pressman and Orr 17). Succession into this stage usually involves a reduction in breathing rate, blood pressure, and pulse, and the entrance to a level of sleep from which waking is more difficult (Epstein and Mardon 15).

Finally, the nature of the last stage in this pattern, REM, distinguishes it as a unique process in itself. Epstein describes this stage as an "active brain in a paralyzed body" (17). During REM, many seemingly unusual occurrences take place: darting eyes; increased body temperature, blood pressure, heart rate, and breathing rate; a highly active sympathetic nervous system; and a temporary paralysis of the majority of the body's muscles (Epstein and Mardon 17). One of the most notable characteristics of this stage lies in its facilitation of both memory and learning. Overall, REM occurs about every 90 minutes throughout a night of sleep, with its duration increasing as the night progresses. While the duration and frequency of each of the five stages differ, a single night of sleep usually involves several cycles. Each cycle, in turn, consists of multiple transitions between the different stages.

Progression through these stages enables the body to carry out several psychological and physiological processes. The consideration of these effects places crucial emphasis on levels of adequate and inadequate sleep. On one hand, adequate amounts of sleep enable the body to restore and revive itself. Modern studies reveal such processing time as an essential aspect to formulating new, long-term memories: "Memory consolidation takes place during sleep through the strengthening of the neural connections that form our memories" (Harvard Medical). This reveals the association between sleep and memory improvement. However, sleep not only aids in memory formation, but it is also shown in several studies to affect physical performance. In the article "Sleep: The Athlete's Steroid," published in the *IDEA Fitness Journal*, Mike Bracko discusses several studies conducted concerning the effects of varying amounts of sleep on an athlete's performance. One such study noted that when researchers increased the length of sleep for members of a swim team to "10 hours per day for 6-7 weeks . . . results showed that the swimmers swam the 15-meter sprint 0.51 seconds faster, reacted 0.15 seconds sooner off the start blocks . . . and increased kick strokes by 5 kicks" (Bracko). These findings reveal the direct relationship between sleep performance in not just sports, but also the physical activities associated with everyday living.

Moreover, sleep's effect on performance may lie in direct relation to the impact it has on the internal body systems. In the *Sleep Disorders Sourcebook*, Sandra Judd explains that sleep affects the endocrine system, the renal system, and the digestive system (9-10). The impact on and regulation of all of these systems ultimately alters the functioning of the entire body. One such example, according to Gerard Lombardo, M.D., in his book *Sleep to Save Your Life,* states, "Tissue cells, which are worn out during the normal wear and tear of living, need sleep to repair themselves" (22). For instance, during sleep, the pituitary gland secretes a substance known as the growth hormone, which promotes the growth and repair of tissue (Epstein and Mardon 16). Therefore, such a seemingly simple task as sleep represents an incredibly complex period in the day during which people unconsciously carry on the diligent work involved in maintaining life.

Inadequate sleep, on the other hand, deprives a person of the above-mentioned restorative properties and the associated impacts they have on the body. According to the article "Healthy Sleep" by Harvard Medical, "A sleep-deprived person cannot focus attention optimally and therefore cannot learn efficiently." This inability ultimately limits the productivity of a person throughout the day, in studying, in performing, or even merely in holding conversations. Not only does lack of sleep lead to drowsiness throughout the day, but it also denies an individual the opportunity he or she needs to process the information and experiences of the day. As previously mentioned, such processing time is the enabling factor in learning and growth.

Another study from *Sleep to Save Your Life* states, "Tests conducted at the Walter Reed Army Institute of Research in Silver Spring, Maryland, show that physical and thinking ability diminishes an average of 25 percent for every 24 hours without sleep" (26). This finding reveals that sleep deprivation hinders both mental and physical competence. Scientists have further supported these findings in studies involving lab rats. Lombardo says that these rats "survive only about five weeks on average when they don't get any REM sleep. When deprived of all sleep stages, they live only about three weeks." (19). Even though such functional decline manifests itself differently in humans, it still poses a serious danger. Epstein describes this negative trend in saying, "Lack of sleep is directly linked to poor health" (5). In other words, inadequate amounts of sleep place individuals in a state of risk, both mentally and physically. Thus, the effects of inadequate sleep over time lead one to an overall lower quality of life.

The fact of the matter is this: sleep remains one of the daily activities in which everyone participates to some degree. Through the progression of technology, a more effective means of studying the brain has added several new dimensions to the study of sleep. Scientists not only look at what specifically occurs during this process, such as the five stages, but they now look beyond to discover the biological activities associated with each stage. Identifying such information enables researchers to improve society's understanding of the importance of sleep and its influence on day-to-day living as a whole.

Works Cited

Bracko, Mike. "Sleep: The Athlete's Steroid." *IDEA Fitness Journal* 10.10 (2013): 44-50. Web. 14 Feb. 2009.

Epstein, Lawrence, and Steven Mardon. *The Harvard Medical School Guide to a Good Night's Sleep.* New York: McGraw-Hill, 2007. Print.

Harvard Medical School. "Sleep, Learning, and Memory." *Healthy Sleep.* Web. 12 Feb. 2014.

Judd, Sandra. *Sleep Disorders Sourcebook: Basic Consumer Health Information about Sleep Disorders, Including Insomnia, Sleep Apnea and Snoring, Jet Lag and Other Circadian Rhythm Disorders, Narcolepsy, and Parasomnias, Such as Sleepwalking and Sleep Paralysis, and Feat.* 3rd ed. Detroit, MI: Omnigraphics, 2010. Print.

Lombardo, Gerard. *Sleep to Save Your Life: The Complete Guide to Living Longer and Healthier Through Restorative Sleep.* NY: Collins, 2005. Print.

Pressman, Mark, and William Orr. Understanding Sleep: *The Evaluation and Treatment of Sleep Disorders.* Washington, DC: American Psychological Association, 1997. Print.

Schenck, Carlos. *Sleep: The Mysteries, the Problems, and the Solutions.* New York: Avery, 2007. Print.

"Foster Care: the Good, the Bad, and the Ugly" by Stephen Combs

Instructor's Notes

This assignment required students to fully explore all sides of an issue while maintaining a neutral point of view. Why might such an exploration be important both inside and outside of the classroom? What other writing genres might require such a stance? What factors would be important when selecting sources for this specific genre?

Writers' Biography

Stephen Combs is a second-year Finance major from Miamisburg, Ohio. Stephen takes academics very seriously. As far as writing goes, he enjoys blogging and writing an occasional poem or two but is not a big fan of academic writing. However, Stephen enjoys a good challenge, and academic writing provides that for him. In his spare time, he enjoys playing most every sport in existence, working, playing the ukulele, and hanging out with friends and family.

Foster Care: the Good, the Bad, and the Ugly

Opinions pertaining to out-of-home care, better known as foster care, tend to vary significantly in the United States. The need for such a system is undeniable, yet many wonder if the federal government is doing too much or too little. Some previously fostered children become valued members of society, while many others find themselves in prisons or on the street. The United States government provides funding and services in order to improve the living situation of maltreated children. One of the ways in which they do this is by placing the mistreated children in foster homes and paying caregivers to provide for the well being of the child or children. The creation of foster care system took place in the early 1960s. However, it was not until the 1970s that the United States government put emphasis on expanding their role in child welfare by implementing policy framework and providing funding (Courtney, Flynn, Beaupré 164). Though there are several strict governmental policies that exist with the intention to protect and enhance the well being of maltreated children, the outcome of the lives of fostered children is wide-ranged.

The Child Abuse Prevention and Treatment Act of 1974 requires all professionals who interact with children to report guardian behavior or signs of guardian behavior that could be considered neglect or child abuse to child protection authorities (Courtney, Flynn, Beaupré 164). Such reports lead to investigation of the suspect situation. The investigation, done by a child protection agency of some sort, results in either no governmental action or the issuance of the maltreated child into the foster care system (Courtney, Flynn, Beaupré 164). According to the United States Department of Health and Human Services, concerned citizens filed 1,820,892 maltreated child reports in 2012, and 678,810 of them uncovered victims of abuse and/or neglect (19). This means that there are approximately nine victimized children for every one thousand total children in the United States. Every one of these abused and/or neglected children is in need of governmental assistance to improve their living situation. Foster care exists to achieve just that, to improve the living situation of maltreated children.

The courts handle the permanent planning for children removed from a living situation that involved maltreatment. The Adoption Assistance and Child Welfare Act of 1980 (Public Law 96-272) is the policy that set the precedent of the court handling the placement of soon to be foster children (Courtney, Flynn, Beaupré 165). If no responsible family member steps up to take custody, the court assigns the victimized child to one of two types of out-of-home options , the first of which is residential care (del Valle 162). Residential care consists of a group of fostered children living together beneath one roof. The homes in which they live in are staffed by paid staff and/or volunteers. Family care is the other variation of out-of-home care. In this style of foster care, a non-kin family assumes the responsibility of caring for the previously neglected youth (del Valle 162). The length of time a child stays in foster care is impossible to predict. The courts may only be place the child in foster care for a few hours or the remainder of their childhood. The state children's welfare agency is required to work on the child's behalf with an overarching goal to achieve one of two outcomes: either the family will be reunified or a complete termination of parental rights will take place (Chittom, Lynn-nore, Wagner, Geraldine 1). With the termination of parental rights, the possibility of adoption is opened.

There are many horror stories and criticisms of foster care as a whole, but judging by the statistics, success often occurs. Fifty-one percent of the children who exited foster care in 2012 left because they had the opportunity to reunite with their parents (Child Welfare Information Gateway 1). Reuniting the child with their family is typically the primary goal of caseworkers (Courtney, Flynn, Beaupré 165). In addition, about half of the children who left foster care in the same year were only a part of the out-of-home system for less than a year (Child Welfare Information Gateway 1). In January of 2000, the Department of Health and Human Services announced the implementation of a new set of guidelines known as the Child and Family Service Reviews. The purpose of these new regulations was to improve the odds of positive outcomes among foster care and other child welfare programs (Chittom, Lynn-nore, Wagner, Geraldine 1). Whether or not these additional rules are doing an adequate job is vague. Regardless, foster care has made a positive impact on the lives of many.

Babe Ruth (one of the greatest professional players of all time) and Eddie Murphy (famous actor/comedian) both spent time in foster homes. Both of them went on to make a positive name for themselves in society. Babe Ruth and Eddie Murphy are by no means the only success stories to come out of foster care. One previously fostered child named Sara declared, "Foster care was one of the best things that ever happened to me " ("Foster Care Success Stories" 1). Sara is currently a successful model ("Foster Care Success Stories" 1).

Sadly, not every fostered child receives the same results as Eddie Murphy, Babe Ruth, or Sara. The placement of an adolescent into residential or family foster care does not guarantee future health and happiness for previously victimized children. Courtney et al. gave the statistic, "24,000 foster youth who 'age out' of care each year are expected to make it on their own long before the vast majority of their peers" (1). "Aging out" too soon is not the only issue that reduces the chances of success in the world for foster children. Some never get over the physical, emotional, and mental trauma they at one time faced (Pecora 6). Others are placed in homes in which their foster parents take very little interest in them (Combs). Occasionally their "caregivers" will even neglect them (Combs).

In the words of Peter Pecora, "Youth in foster care and adults who formerly were placed in care (foster care alumni) have disproportionately high rates of emotional and behavioral disorders" (6). Most every child who was previously or is currently a part of the foster care system has lived a tremendously tough life, filled with emotional scars (Pecora 6). Unfortunately, in addition to the baggage the child caries into the out-of-home living situation, mental and behavioral health of fostered children often tend to decrease during the time spent in foster care (Cunningham and Finlay 765). The level of severity among these cases varies greatly. It could be as minor as a below normal self-esteem, or as major as complete defiance to all authority to the point of violence. However, the issues are severe enough that approximately eighty percent of foster children who have a mental or behavioral condition are in need of intervention (Pecora 6).

Other children who were rescued from unhealthy situations and placed into the foster care system bounce from one physically unhealthy situation to another, meaning the child goes from being victimized in their original home to being abused in their assigned foster home. According to the United States Department of Health and Human Services, foster parents neglect their foster children in less than one percent of out-of-home care situations (50). This statistic baffled Eastway Corporation counselor, Anna Combs. In her seven years as a counselor, she has encountered many neglected foster kids. The foster parent(s) of these children provide a roof for them, but that is about as far as the caring goes. These insufficient caregivers misuse the money they receive for fostering the children on themselves or on their biological children.

Few would argue the fact that foster children tend to struggle in the academic realm. A 2007 study performed by Courtney et al. consisted of interviewing young, previously fostered adults (5). The study found that only who had a high school diploma or GED (Courtney et al. 5). In the same study, only point nine percent indicated they had a two-year college degree, and not one person interviewed had a four-year college degree (Courtney, Dworsky, Cusick, Havlicek, Perez, and Keller 5). Though education is not the only sign of success, these statistics certainly are disturbing. In America's current economic state, jobs are scarce. With little to no higher education, finding a suitable workplace is practically impossible.

Foster care is a prominent part of modern society; it is so prominent that the US government has established many rules, regulations, and processes pertaining to it. With the number of currently fostered children increasing each year, it is apparent that there will always be a need for such a system. Foster care, as a whole, is difficult to label. It is easy to point out and focus on either positives or negatives. Foster care has helped and continues to help many people. Most likely, it has saved lives. On the other hand, foster care has given and continues to give many children psychological disorders or assisted in the worsening of previously established psychological disorders in an abundance of other children. Some previously fostered adults achieve great successes. Many others are either homeless or in jail. The outcomes of the lives of foster children are truly all over the board.

Works Cited

Combs, Anna. Phone interview. February 10.

Courtney, Mark, Amy Dworsky, Gretchen Cusick, Judy Havlicek, Alfred Perez, and Tom Keller. "Child Welfare Outcomes 2008–2011: Report to Congress." *Home.* Chapin Hall, Dec. 2007. Web. 13 Feb. 2014.

"Child Maltreatment 2012." *Reports.* Child Welfare Information Gateway, 17 Dec. 2013. Web. 13 Feb. 2014.

Chittom, Lynn-noreWagner, Geraldine. "Foster Children Programs: An Overview." *Points Of View: Foster Children Programs* (2013): 1. Points of View Reference Center. Web. 9 Feb. 2014.

Courtney, Mark, Robert J. Flynn, and Joël Beaupré. "Overview Of Out Of Home Care In The USA And Canada." *Psychosocial Intervention / Intervencion Psicosocial* 22.3 (2013): 163-173. *Academic Search Complete.* Web. 9 Feb. 2014.

Cunningham, Scott, and Keith Finlay. "Parental Substance Use And Foster Care: Evidence From Two Methamphetamine Supply Shocks." *Economic Inquiry* 51.1 (2013): 764-782. *Academic Search Complete.* Web. 13 Feb. 2014.

del Valle, Jorge F. "Out Of Home Care In Child Protection: An International Overview." *Psychosocial Intervention / Intervencion Psicosocial* 22.3 (2013): 161-162. *Academic Search Complete.* Web. 9 Feb. 2014.

"Foster Care Stories." *Home.* D.A. Blodgett - St. John's. Web. 13 Feb. 2014.

Pecora, Peter J, et al. "Mental Health Services For Children Placed In Foster Care: An Overview Of Current Challenges." *Child Welfare* 88.1 (2009): 5-26. *MEDLINE with Full Text.* Web. 9 Feb. 2014.

United States Department of Health and Human Services. *Child Maltreatment* 2012. Children's Bureau, 17 Dec. 2013. Web. 10 Feb. 2014.

"Tuning In or Tuning Out?"
by Lynn David Long

Instructor's Notes

This informative, expository essay by Lynn David Long asks the question, "Is Radio Dead?" Although you many never have considered this question before, did the author successfully pique your interest in this topic? Why or Why not? This essay also includes an annotated bibliography. Have you ever written one before? What do you suppose the purpose is? What do you think about the quality of David's sources?

Writers' Biography

David Long is a sophomore Applied Communications major with an emphasis in broadcasting and public communication. Besides hiking the mountains around his home in Western North Carolina, David loves reading, writing and sports. He is a member of the Cedarville University competitive speech team and serves as the music director of Resound Radio, the student radio station at Cedarville.

Tuning In or Tuning Out?

The place that I now call my office, relaxation space, and second home is the student radio station at Cedarville University, otherwise known as Resound Radio. It is a place that represents more than a job; it is an outlet for my voice, and fulfills a desire for belonging. Through my current studies and career goals, I am preparing for a life in the business of radio. The difficulty attached to this career path is the seemingly wide belief that radio is no longer a viable media option: that people are not interested in radio anymore. This would affect the future of the industry, would it not? If people are not interested they stop listening and then revenue for stations would deteriorate, rendering radio personnel jobless and aspiring DJs pursuing new career paths. So why do I even continue this pursuit of radio, a growing passion of mine? With the historical, technological, and personal implications associated with radio seemingly going by the wayside, it begs the question: Is radio dead? This essay examines the relevancy of radio in the modern media setting by exploring some aspects of the birth and history of radio, certain characteristics that makes radio unique, and its current and future standing in the media market. Radio is a means of media, by way of local and national stations, a listener can tune in to any variety of music, talk shows, sports broadcasts, and news programs. The radio industry has had an effect on media. In order to understand how radio has affected media, historical aspects of the industry must first be examined. Next, the reasons why radio appeals to listeners as a media outlet must be assessed. Once the history and the appeal of radio is grasped, the future of radio can be considered. It is in this order that the topic will be explained.

Radio is connected to communication and technology, which in turn is connected to science. The development of science leads to innovation and creation in new forms of technology and communication. In order to appreciate the birth of radio, an appreciation for the development of the science behind the communication outlet should be obtained first. This understanding that technology and communication are not separated from each other is an important factor to consider in radio development as a media outlet. The driving force behind technology and communication is science, for as science improves understanding and developments in technology so does technology improve communication (Barboutis 156).

The development of broadcast radio was a gradual process, as the audience had to learn to listen to this form of communication. "The transformation of a radio listener to a fan or a community occurred slowly. Listeners reported that sometimes their older family members steadfastly refused to listen to the radio, favoring other forms of entertainment" (MacLennan 313-314). As MacLennan shares in her article on the development of the Canadian radio audience, once listeners learned the technology and prepared their schedules around the broadcasted programs, casual listeners became fans (325). As families began listening together, table top and floor model radios became popular in households, fueling the continued growth. Canadians loved their sports, especially hockey, and the ability to hear games broadcast across the country in the 1920s and

156

1930s helped to spur more popularity for the medium (MacLennan 319). Through the development of radio in Canada, the ideas presented by Barboutis seem quite fitting. "As reception range grew, radio receivers in most homes improved as radio became a vehicle for information and entertainment, no longer a piece of technology for experimentation" (MacLennan 316). Technology was an early fascination with the radio audience and once they grew accustomed to the technology, the audience expanded. Barboutis explains that technology and communication are inseparable and are bounded by science (156). Early development in Canadian radio showcase this concept by the process of growth in the Canadian listening audience.

The history of radio grew from the development of technology, which improved communication and was founded by science. As seen in the growth of early Canadian listeners, once the technology was understood, the radio became part of the household. With its birth in science, radio made an impact in communication and drew attention from listeners. What did audiences hear in radio that kept making them listen? The appeal, or reasons for listening provide intriguing clues to radio's current relevancy.

> Canadian radio listeners became part of their immediate communities when theycongregated in groups to listen to their favorite programs, such as hockey, even before every home was equipped with a radio receiver. As their listening became a daily ritual that was taken for granted, the audience or individual listeners learned to become parts of larger groups of fans and enthusiasts across Canada and North America. (MacLennan 325)

Radio created connections for individuals, families, and communities. Listeners received something special from radio programs, a sense of home as described in Anne Karpf's article. "Indeed, even when the radio voice is at its most instrumental- spelling out wind direction, precipitation, sea conditions in the shipping forecast- it has the capacity to engender a deep attachment" (Karpf 61). The deep attachment is described as homeliness, a feeling of comfort and familiarity. When a listener connects with a familiar station, music, or a favorite radio voice, they want to return to that feeling of homeliness. These feelings stem from various situations, whether it is a connection through sports, music genre, or talk shows, which ultimately came from a desire to be contained. Containment is described as the consoling power a radio voice has over the fears and frustrations of a listener. The voice can't be seen, only heard. It is this fact that Karpf believes connects us so powerfully to radio, because it is similar to hearing our mother's voice while in the womb (Karpf 63). As our bad feelings could be controlled by our mother at an early age, so can the radio voice contain our bad feelings as a listener. Though this power of radio can and has been misused, the listener does enjoy this connection and returns to it to hear more.

Radio's draw does come from content as well. Programs like sports, music, talk shows and news broadcasts are defining features of radio. Karpf suggests that even beyond the general connections like listening as a family or following a sports team the listener develops a sense of homeliness when accustomed to a particular radio voice. Other attractions for radio is the use of modern technology to promote connections to listeners. Modern radio is including mobile technology to encourage participation in programming, providing unique ways for listeners to connect with radio. A case study performed by Rey G. Rosales, which examined the way two different radio stations used mobile technology to encourage audience participation, showcases some ways that radio stations and listeners are connecting using various technology. Three distinct areas of participation were discovered by Rosales; social interaction, entertainment, and social contact and surveillance of the environment (255). Uses such as text alerts, social media, traditional call-ins, and website use were ways that audience members used mobile technology to participate in one or more of the three areas of participation (Rosales 255). Not only does a listener have an emotional connection with radio, but a continually growing physical connection through technology as well.

This essay has explored some historical aspects of radio and certain emotional and technological connections radio has with its audience. The understanding of how a listenership develops and then stays with radio is necessary for exploring the relevancy of radio today. Since this has been accomplished, it is now appropriate to explore the question at hand: Is radio dead?

"The percentage of people who listen to the AM/FM radio each week remained essentially unchanged in 2012, compared with figures from a decade earlier. In 2012, 92% of Americans age 15 or older listened to the radio at least weekly, essentially the same as it was a decade earlier (94%)" (Mitchell Journalism.org). These are fascinating facts to consider in a modern radio world. In roughly a decade, listenership numbers have dropped only slightly. The Pew Research Center's Project for Excellence in Journalism's State of the Media report records more intriguing statistics. One example is the usage of online radio by listeners has grown rapidly in the past couple of years, roughly 39% in 2012 compared to 27% in 2010 (Mitchell Journalism.org). Talk radio continues to be very popular, with conservative talk show host Rush Limbaugh boasting the most listened to show in 2012 with 15 million listeners (Mitchell Journalism.org). Satellite radio also continues to remain prominent among listeners as SiriusXM® attracted a record number of subscribers in 2012: 2 million new subscribers bringing the total to 23.9 million (Mitchell Journalism.org). There is large quantity and growth in radio listenership in 2012, which suggests that radio has a place in our current age.

These numbers show a common theme of use of radio as a means of media in this current age. This is a powerful discovery, as the belief that radio is dead appears to be untrue. "…technology and communication do not operate independently of one another, but instead are bound together via the influence of the field of science" (Barboutis 156). As technology is used by radio to enhance listenership, communication grows with that listenership. Additionally, online and mobile radio is projected to see the steadiest increases over the years ahead (Mitchell Journalism.org). "From the standpoint of uses and gratification theory, it is clear that the radio stations examined and analyzed in this study were trying to expand the ways they can interact and engage their listeners and thereby increase their loyal following. One of the ways to do that is through the use of mobile technology and via the embedded social media platforms" (Rosales 255). As seen by the case study and the statistics, technological improvements and advances are areas of growth for radio. As defined earlier, technology and communication are inseparable, and radio is a communication outlet improving in many areas with technology. This would suggest that radio's relevancy in today's media is not only vast, but also growing. However, there are certain factors to consider that could speak to the potential for radio to decline in coming years.

The first consideration is the overall earnings for radio

stations increased by very small amounts and only with aid of election advertisements (Mitchell Journalism.org). Consider this: if radio needed help to improve earnings from election advertisements, it could be a problem for continued earnings in the future when elections are not taking place; which means losing buying power for new technology and improvement. The FCC, the Federal Communications Commission, created a task force in 2003 to explore the possibility that bigger network stations and satellite radio companies were encroaching on local radio stations and their ability to compete in a crowded market (Sauls and Greer 37). This is an issue because local radio plays an important role in communities. Aside from just giving the weather and traffic for local areas, the listenership does make connections with particular radio voices, which has shown positive and powerful impacts (Karpf 62). However, with network stations buying many smaller stations and radio frequencies and satellite radio drawing more listeners, local radio stations begin to lose their ability to make connections and lose the audience (Sauls and Greer 37). The hope is the FCC will provide some protection for radio and localism, but as of now is arguably failing to do so adequately. "With the FCC showing no indication of revisiting localism in any substantial form, it could very well be up to the radio industry itself to the take the lead" (Sauls and Greer 48). There is some danger for the radio industry, which must be considered when examining whether its relevancy as an industry is valid.

There is always potential for growth in radio because radio was created through technology. Technology is connected to communication and they are bounded by science (Barboutis 156). The largest increases for radio have been in online and satellite radio (Mitchell Journalism.org). Social media has become a factor in increasing radio presence, but radio stations could provide more outlets for social media use. "They need to push the envelope quite a bit more by letting listeners and fans of the station become an active partner in the conversation and in the content creation process whether on-air and especially on the web" (Rosales 256). The fact there is room for improvement should be testament for potential growth.

This essay sought to explore the relevancy of radio in the modern media market by examining historical aspects that brought radio to life, qualities that make radio appealing to audiences, and data and insights that speak to its current standing and future as a media outlet. By understanding the connection between technology and communication, the appeal of technology and broadcasted information, connections with the radio voice, current trends in the radio market, and possible factors that could lead to a decline of radio use, the issue of the relevancy of radio can be answered. Data indicates that radio is not dying, but perhaps changing. With 92% of Americans still listening to FM/AM radio stations, it is a safe assumption that radio is still a major part of the media market (Mitchell Journalism.org). What lies ahead for radio is uncertain, as the problems of declining localism and possible loss in revenue does hang over the industry's head. However, with increases in listeners among the channels of online and satellite radio, there are still areas of progress to appreciate. As stations learn to use various tools, like social media, effective improvements can still be made in the industry. Radio is very much alive and a large part of our everyday media. Listeners are still tuning in.

Bibliography

Barboutis, Christos. "The Birth Of Radio Broadcasting: The Matrix Of Science, Technology And Communication In The Western World." *Radio Journal: International Studies In Broadcast & Audio Media* 11.2 (2013): 155-168. Web. 25 Feb. 2014.

Karpf, Anne. "The Sound Of Home? Some Thoughts On How The Radio Voice Anchors, Contains And Sometimes Pierces." *Radio Journal: International Studies In Broadcast & Audio Media* 11.1 (2013): 59-73. *Communication & Mass Media Complete*. Web. 25 Feb. 2014.

MacLennan, Anne F. "Learning To Listen: Developing The Canadian Radio Audience In The 1930S." *Journal Of Radio & Audio Media* 20.2 (2013): 311-326. *Communication & Mass Media Complete*. Web. 26 Feb. 2014.

Rosales, R. G. "Citizen Participation and the Uses of Mobile Technology in Radio Broadcasting." *Telematics and Informatics* 30.3 (2013): 252-257. *SCOPUS*. Web. 26 Feb. 2014.

Santhanam, Laura, Amy Mitchell, and Kenny Olmstead. "Audio: By the Numbers." *Journalism.org.* Ed. Amy Mitchell. The Pew Research Center's Project for Excellence in Journalism, 2014. Web. 25 Feb. 2014.

Sauls, Samuel J., and Danny Greer. "Radio And Localism: Has The FCC Dropped The Ball?" *Journal Of Radio Studies* 14.1 (2007): 37-48. *Communication & Mass Media Complete.* Web. 26 Feb. 2014.

"Black and Blue: Dispelling the Myth of Racism in Avatar" by Leah Rachel Bode

Instructor's Notes

The position paper required students to defend a position about a film of their choice from a group of instructor-selected films. Though the thesis did not have to be limited to one sentence, it was required to state the student's position and to forecast the paper's direction. Students were to incorporate various kinds of evidence and to acknowledge and counter opposing arguments. In her paper Leah Rachel chose to defend Avatar against claims of implicit racism. Locate her thesis, and notice how its "forecast" section actually outlines the paper's organization and development. Note also how Leah Rachel carefully explains and then refutes opposing arguments before establishing support for her position about the film. Stylistically, Leah Rachel's paper is replete with vivid word choices: circle some of those that you find especially strong.

Writers' Biography

Leah Rachel Bode will be a senior nursing major at Cedarville University. After graduating, she hopes to pursue midwifery and one day serve God as a medical missionary. She loves the Lord, babies, friends and scrapbooking.

Black and Blue: Dispelling the Myth of Racism in Avatar

In 2009, James Cameron's *Avatar* stunned the world with its brilliantly-crafted animation, groundbreaking effects, and cutting-edge technology. Because *Avatar* demanded more than $230 million and four years of arduous labor to complete, it is no surprise that it received three Oscars in addition to fifty-four other awards (Ebert, "Avatar"). Taking place in 2154, the story focuses on the indigenous population called the Na'vi who lives harmoniously on the planet of Pandora. When word reaches Earth that Pandora possesses unobtainium, the rock that can sell for $20 million a kilo, scientists and military personnel attack the planet.

Disguised in an Avatar body, Jake (the main character) befriends the natives with the goal of securing the precious rock. As time will tell, however, Jake's interactions with the Na'vi people radically transform his world. Surprisingly, despite its immense success, critics have pointed their fingers at the film, labeling it a "racist" "Pocahontas story" (Washington). Although James Cameron's *Avatar* contains stereotypes, the typical "superior-versus-inferior" conflict, and a "white savior," the film does not communicate a message of racism. In fact, several details within the movie blatantly challenge ethnocentrism, imperialism and cruelty. Pandora (the Na'vi homeland) far surpasses Earth with its breathtaking beauty, and it transforms and enlightens the miserable characters arriving from Earth. Although Jake does lead the Na'vi tribe to victory, he continuously relies on the chief's daughter to train him and, in several instances, save his life. Finally, in a crushing blow to the racism accusation, Jake eventually abandons his white race, morphing completely into a full-blooded Na'vi.

Of course, critics do cite valid arguments to support their accusations of the film. One critic in particular, Mitu Sengupta, argues strongly that the message of *Avatar* is blatantly racist (413). To begin with, the movie does contain several stereotypes and clichés. As in so many other films, the "white men" are brutal, ignorant, and heartless, with no regard for suffering. They refer to the Na'vi as "blue monkeys" and "fly-bitten savages that live in a tree" (Cameron). The animation directors portray the Na'vi people with stereotypical African and Indian features, such as tribal jewelry, dreadlocks, mohawks, and feathers in their hair. Portrayed as animalistic, the natives hiss, growl, and sport cat-like eyes and tails. Critics question Cameron's stereotypical portrayal of the natives, along with his decision to cast African-American and Latino actors as Na'vi characters (Washington). Sengupta in particular refers to the "white man messiah" as the most supportive element for ethnocentrism, objecting strongly to the fact that the Na'vi seem unable to save themselves (413). Actress Robinne Lee comments, "It's really upsetting in many ways. It would be nice if we could save ourselves" (Washington). Although many argue that Cameron's film should be rejected for its messages of racism and imperialism, several details from the film disprove this position.

Throughout *Avatar,* it is clearly Cameron's intent to

164

portray the land of Pandora and the Na'vi people as superior to Earth and its inhabitants. In contrast to the intriguing world of Pandora, Jake's spaceship is unappealing and drab, lacking beauty and color. The Marines and scientists rip each other to shreds with their sarcastic and bitter comments, creating a destructive and degrading atmosphere. In contrast, the world of Pandora is magical and enchanting with its glowing vegetation, misty waterfalls, lush ferns, and psychedelic plants. It appears as though a rainbow melted over Pandora, dousing the creatures and natives with vibrant hues of cobalt blue and mossy green. Unlike the team from earth, the Na'vi people extend friendship to Jake and create a sense an atmosphere of and acceptance. Throughout the film, the visual artists purposefully contrast Jake's hopeless surroundings of his spaceship to the intriguing and iridescent world of Pandora.

Discrediting the racism charges even further, *Avatar* suggests that Pandora's power cleanses and renews minds that have been "poisoned" by earth. Although Jake and Grace lead miserable lives at the beginning of the film, both are transformed by Pandora as they spend more time in the cleansing environment. While on earth, Jake suffers from much from sorrow and heartache. Paralyzed and confined to a wheelchair, he is unable to move freely or keep pace with the other marines. In addition to his physical limitations, he is also tethered by emotional baggage as a result of the death of his twin brother. Lacking passion, contentment, and friendship, he views himself as "just another dumb grunt" (Cameron). When he first arrives in Pandora, he stands out sorely against the backdrop of this captivating land, taunting the flora and fauna, treading on the natives' tails, and stumbling into perilous situations. Because of his arrogant disrespect and inconsiderate behavior, the Na'vi people greet him with hostility. But as time elapses, Pandora's magic penetrates his heart and frees him, both physically (paralysis has no power in Pandora) and emotionally (Jake finds friendship and acceptance in the Na'vi tribe). Believing that Pandora is superior to Earth, Jake realizes, "Everything is backwards now. Like out there is the true world and in here is the dream" (Cameron). The testy, miserable Grace Augustine also experiences renewal in this nirvana. In the beginning of the film, this demanding, acidic, disrespectful woman has heartened her heart to the plight of the Na'vi people. Her only concern lies with obtaining the prize, no matter the cost or loss of life. However, her callous heart softens while in Pandora and soon overflows with compassion for the victims. When Grace finally awakens to the destruction looming over the Na'vi tribe, she pleads with her cruel leader Quaritch, "You need to wake up. The wealth of the world is not in the ground. You need to understand them!" (Cameron). Throughout the film, Pandora works like a poultice to draw out the poisons from Earth, healing Jake and Grace.

Despite these facts, however, charges against *Avatar* continue. Upset by the fact that the indigenous population cannot save themselves and instead rely on Jake to lead them, audience members cite this "white man messiah" element as the greatest indicator of racism. But they deny the fact that, although Jake does step in to lead the native people to victory, he relies extensively on the Na'vi woman who has stolen his heart. It is only because of Neytiri's training and guidance that Jake learns to hunt, speak the native language, and survive off the land. In fact, in the storyline she saves his life on three separate occasions. Without Neytiri's intervention, Jake's first encounter with Pandora's vicious creatures would have cost him his life. At the end of the movie, the fierce heroine battles Quaritch on Jake's behalf and also rescues her unconscious lover from suffocation. In fact, it is Neytiri's arrow that pierces Quaritch's heart, saving Pandora and the entire Na'vi race from destruction.

Delivering the final blow to *Avatar's* racist accusations, Jake utterly abandons his status as a 6-foot Caucasian man and embraces life as a full-blooded Na'vi. In Pandora, the natives rescue Jake's spirit from his crippled human body, magically transporting it into an agile, gorgeous Na'vi form. This dramatic twist suggests that joining the indigenous race brings more pleasure and fulfillment than continuing to live as a Caucasian individual, which clearly contradicts the typical ethnocentric position.

When James Cameron released *Avatar,* many critics pointed their fingers and labeled his film racist; however, its messages advocate quite the opposite. The movie cries out against imperialism, encourages Americans to embrace differences among races, warns against the dangers of technology, and applauds environmentalism. The movie raises thought-provoking questions, such as, "How well do we as Americans respect other cultures and the differences within them? Are we allowing arrogance to blind us to the lessons and blessings found in other races?" Through the stunning film *Avatar,* James Cameron paints a diverse and colorful painting of America, blending together hues of brown, black....and just a hint of blue.

Works Cited

"Avatar." IMDb. 18 Dec. 2009. Web. 16 Oct. 2012.

Cameron, James, dir. Avatar Perf. Sam Worthington, Zoe Saldana, and Stephen Lang, 20th Century Fox, 2009. DVD.

Ebert, Roger. "Avatar." *Chicago Sun-Times.* Sun-Times Media, LLC, 2009. Web. 16 Oct. 2012.

Sengupta, Mitu. "Race Relations Light Years from Earth." *Signs of Life in the USA*. Ed. Denise B.Wydra, et al. Boston: Bedford/ St. Martin's, 2012. 412-416. Book.

Washington, Jesse. "'Avatar' Critics See Racist Theme." *Huffington Post*, 2010. Web. 4 Oct. 2012.

"Solving the Palestinian Refugee Crisis"
by Emily Guilliams

Instructor's Notes

For this essay, the rhetorical situation called for Emily to convert research originally gathered for an informative essay into a persuasive, argument essay. To accomplish this, she first had to "listen in to the dialogue" concerning the plight of the Palestinian refugees, learn about their current situation, and then find an argument within the dialogue that she could speak to. Notice that she had to be careful not just to present information about the refugees' suffering. While describing the issue does provide pathos for her essay, she went beyond that description to an argument for a specific solution.

Writers' Biography

Emily Guilliams is a second year International Studies major. She loves writing, but she believes commas are an unsolvable enigma. In her spare time, she dreams of traveling the world and roots for Cleveland sports teams to be decent.

Solving the Palestinian Refugee Crisis

For over sixty years, political leaders, and academics have discussed it. Countless books have addressed it. The United Nations (UN) has issued resolutions about it, but the debate about the plight of Palestinians refugees continues. This situation contains many highly debatable issues. These include questions of who is responsible for the refugees and what solutions are viable economically, politically, and legally. While the length and magnitude of this debate make it seem impossible to resolve satisfactorily for all parties, many world leaders still try. The reality of millions of Palestinian refugees living in limbo along with the desire for lasting peace should inspire commitment to a possible solution. After a consideration of rights, historical events, and the current situation, the most realistic plan for solving the Palestinian refugee problem is for Arab governments to grant Palestinian refugees, who reside inside their territory, citizenship and integrate them as soon as possible.

The Palestinian refugees' suffering, caused by the loss of identity and prolonged human rights violations, should lead world leaders to demand action. For over sixty years, the Palestinian's fates have been a bargaining chip leaving many to an undesirable fate. Many of these Palestinians, who fled Israel in 1948, "left behind their belongings and expected to return to their homes within days or weeks" (Marx). When this did not happen, a "demoralizing process of pauperization" (Nachmias) occurred. A reversal of this process has not happened for many Palestinian refugees. Some have been doomed to a life "in squalid camps for decades" (Nachmias). This is not an acceptable human rights situation. The Universal Declaration of Human Rights in 1948 stated, "Everyone has the right to a standard of living adequate for the health and well-being of himself and of his family" (Leckie 3); however, many Palestinians have discovered how easily neglected and manipulated the rights of those without a state are. Some Arab countries have promoted the idea that "improving Palestinian conditions and giving them basic rights would facilitate their full integration in the host society and thus weaken their Palestinian identity" (El-Abed 531). This would supposedly lead to the Palestinians abandoning their right of return. Actual fieldwork, conducted among Palestinians in Egypt, shows that the "major factors encouraging Palestinians to hide or even lose their sense of Palestinian identity, are the deprivation of basic rights and the uncertainties arising from their precarious legal status" (El-Abed 532). This denial of basic rights is demonstrated by the Lebanese government, who "assigned [Palestinian refugees] the legal status of foreigners, which has negatively affected their rights to health care, social services, education and property ownership" (Ibrahim 83). This has occurred despite the 1951 Refugee Convention giving refugees the right to provisions such as aid, employment, education, and the justice system (Holzer 842). Long-term refugee status has left Palestinians vulnerable to political manipulation, rights violations, and economic discrimination.

In addition to this vulnerability, refugee status is creating a dangerous culture of short-term benefits that damages long-term solutions. The actions of refugees' grandchildren are an example of this. Even those grandchildren who live in "relative comfort" still usually "list themselves as refugees" because Palestinians fortunate enough to be settled and involved in society still "enjoy the monetary and other benefits granted them by" the United Nations Relief and Works Agency (UNRWA) (Bartal). According to a 1968 study, many Palestinian refugees who were not originally located in refugee camps later moved in to them (Marx). This happened because in a refugee camp "[t]hey paid no rent and no municipal taxes and their water supply and sanitation were free" (Marx). These Palestinians have a special UN agency, the UNRWA dedicated to their welfare (Bartal); however, the UNRWA, itself, faces a similar conflict of short-term welfare that complicates solutions. This is because the UNRWA hires almost entirely out of the refugee population, with a continued "demand by Palestinians to increase staffing and thereby provide employment" (Marx). This set-up means that a resolution to the Palestinian refugee problem would eliminate the need for the UNRWA (Marx). This would in turn eliminate "the largest employer in the West Bank and Gaza Strip" (Marx). This creates a clear conflict of interest, which along with the benefits and drawbacks of refugee status have led many refugee camps to become permanent (Marx). This is not completely negative. Palestinians have "invested capital in improvements," and currently refugee camps can be "among the better lower-class urban quarters" (Marx). Nonetheless, the permanency of refugee camps inhibits possible solutions. Evidences of this is seen in the "close-knit social networks" and situations that cause refugees to "not wish to leave their property, livelihoods, and friends in order to be resettled," and help continue the "refugee existence" on through the generations (Marx). While the improvement of conditions for Palestinian refugees is good, its effects and the UNRWA's conflicted position threaten to replace a permanent resolution with a stateless status passed on through generations.

If the international community is going to solve this problem while it is still possible, world leaders should agree upon Israel's right to a Jewish-majority and therefore its justification to refuse the return of Palestinians. If all the refugees were to return, it would end the Jewish majority. Many see this an encouraging possibility. Israel's tactics in preserving its Jewish majority are compared by critics "to Nazi Germany and apartheid South Africa" (Karsh 320), but those who say that there is no need for a Jewish-majority state ignore history. The establishment of the state of Israel gave proof of the dangerous reality that exists for Jewish people. During the United Nations debate about establishing a Jewish state, only two years after the Second World War and the Holocaust ended, the Arab League's Secretary-General Abdel Rahman Azzam warned of a possible "war of extermination and momentous massacre" against the Jews (321). In the years following the 1948 birth of Israel, "nearly all of the 850,000-strong Jewish population living in Arab states" fled or were forced from their homes (Bartal). Many of these Jewish communities "predated the Muslim conquest of the Middle East by hundreds of years" (Bartal). Threats of extermination have continued through many Middle Eastern leaders and groups, including "the Palestine Liberation Organization (PLO) whose publicly stated goal since its creation in 1964 has been the destruction of the state of Israel" (Karsh 321). These threats have not stopped. Recently, Mahmoud Ahmadinejad, then president of Iran, declared that Israel should "be 'wiped off the map'" (321). Even some western academics have voiced their support for "the actual elimination of the Jewish state" (322). History demonstrates these threats are not new or going anywhere. In light of this reality, Israel's position, which has remained the same since its first Prime Minister Ben-Gurion articulated "that a real solution of the refugee problem lay in the resettlement of the refugees in Arab states" (Nachmias), is not going to change. In addition, while Israel protects its ethnic majority, the country declared at its founding the goal of "absolute social and political equality of rights for all its citizens" (Karsh 333). In fact, Israel gave its Arab population "educational, cultural, judicial, and religious autonomy," and this part of the population has made steady economic and lifestyle improvements since the creation of Israel (333). Now Israel's Arab male population enjoys a life expectancy over eight years longer than the average Middle Eastern man does (333). These facts are in opposition to the claim that Israel is a modern day apartheid. This historical persecution and these recent threats should cause world leaders to accept Israel and its rights. Thus, in order to move forward with Palestinian resettlement, world leaders need to accept Israel's right to refuse the return of Palestinians.

However, even if leaders acknowledge the need for a Jewish-state, many Arab countries and Palestinians will still claim that Israel is responsible for the fate of the Palestinian refugees. While they are quick to fix blame for the plight of the Palestinians, Arabs and Palestinians usually ignore the parallel displacement of Jewish people. Because of the declaration of a Jewish State and the war that followed in 1948, approximately "700,000 Palestinians sought refuge in neighboring countries" (Peteet 3). In contrast, after the establishment of Israel 850,000 Jewish people were "expelled or escaped" from Arab countries (Bartal). The majority went to Israel where they "were settled during the 1950s in transit camps" (Bartal). Instead of maintaining these camps, Israel transitioned them "into development towns or neighborhoods" (Bartal). To explain the difference between the fates of Jewish and Palestinian refugees, many Palestinian advocates "argue that the Arab states were not empowered to represent them" and "claim … that Jews who emigrated did so because of Zionist manipulation rather than persecution and harassment" (Bartal). Historical evidence does not support this assertion of Zionist influence as the main reason for Jewish migration (Bartal). This evidence includes Syria passing a law that froze "all Jewish bank accounts," Jewish people "being attacked by Arab mobs" in Egypt, and "a horrible pogrom [organized attack on a certain religious or ethnic group] in the Libyan capital of Tripoli" (Bartal). This population exchange suggests a shift of the responsibility for the Palestinians to the Arab countries that expelled or lost, depending on interpretation of events, hundreds of thousands of Jews. Furthermore, when politicians call for the payment of losses from Israel to the displaced Palestinians, they overlook, purposely or accidently, the property exchange that occurred between Israel and Arab countries. Estimated at the equivalent of 3.4 billion dollars, the value of property left behind in Israel by Palestinians is dwarfed by "the worth of Jewish assets left behind," which were "estimated in 2003 at over $100 billion" (Bartal). A possible explanation for this disparity in property losses is that the population exchange was largely "an inequitable exchange of educated and often prosperous Jews for a population of uneducated refugees with no professional skills" (Bartal). These statistics regarding population and property indicate that the international community should not hold Israel mainly or solely responsible for the Palestinians' fate. The Arab countries of the Middle East lost large Jewish populations. These Jews were in general taken in and aided by Israel; thus, it is reasonable to infer, that these Arab countries should bear substantial responsibility for the settlement and aid of those Palestinians who fled Israel.

The Arab nations' responsibility extends to resettling the refugees, a solution once considered inevitable. In the 1950s, most authorities saw the solution of resettlement and integration, rejected now by most, as the probable outcome. Much of the arguments for and against the Palestinian's right of return come from the UN General Assembly resolutions 194 and 394 (Romirowsky). These resolutions declared the need for "the reintegration of the refuges into the economic life of the Near East, either by repatriation or resettlement" (Joffe). As soon as 1951, the reintegration of Palestinians refugees "was understood in diplomatic circles exclusively as resettlement" (Joffe). The U.N. Secretary-General Trygve Lie's hope was that "refugees [would] lead an independent life in countries which have given them shelter" (Nachmias). Because of the poor economic statuses of Arab countries, the plan was to "offer the Arab governments vast resources" in exchange for integrating the refugees (Nachimas). Originally, "Arab states vehemently opposed resolution 194 and voted unanimously against it," but many Arab countries quietly agreed to resettle Palestinian refugees with the incentive of western economic aid (Bartal). Unfortunately due to a combination of governments' opposition, failure of funding to materialize, and a "misperception of the ultimate goals" these resettlement efforts did not solve the refugee problem (Nachimas). Despite the ultimate failure of these efforts, the fact that sixty years ago knowledgeable officials had accepted that Palestinians were not going to return to Israel supports resettlement as the most viable option.

Additionally, resettlement is realistic because the population of Palestinians in need of resettlement is more manageable than various estimates would suggest. The UNRWA has repeatedly expanded the definition of refugee to now when it includes Palestinians "who lost both their homes and means of livelihood as a result of the 1948 Arab-Israeli conflict" and their descendants (Joffe). Under this definition, there are close to five million Palestinian refugees. This number fails to account for the integration of Palestinians in Arab societies. While the resettlement efforts of the 1950s overall unsuccessful, it did result in the "resettling hundreds of thousands of refugees in Jordan, Gaza, and the West Bank" (Nachmias). Since most Palestinian refugees have integrated at least somewhat, "only a quarter of the descendants of the Palestinian refugees still live in camps, the majority of these in Lebanon" (Bartal). Furthermore, the "majority of refugees and their descendants listed with UNRWA currently live in Jordan" (Bartal). Over two million refugees are registered in Jordan along with one and a half million other Palestinians, of which ninety-five percent "hold Jordanian citizenship and enjoy its benefits" (Bartal); therefore, the number of Palestinian refugees that would need help resettling is a very small percentage of this five million. The granting of citizenship, which would secure equal rights and identity for Palestinians, would not be significant change for most Arab countries; however, an exception is Lebanon where Palestinian refugees "are barred from numerous professions" (Marx). In contrast, to the perception that millions of refugees are destitute sitting in camps waiting to return to Israel, the facts actually point to a smaller, solvable problem.

Even with this historical acceptance and virtual assimilation of many Palestinians, Palestinian refugees and their advocates claim "the right of Palestinian refugees to return to their homes [remains] firmly anchored in international law" (Weaver 8). Although authorities closer to the establishment of laws, which are used to justify the right of return, accepted the legality of resettlement, actions of the UN, UNRWA, and Arab leaders have led to "the misrepresentation of resolution 194 as solely aimed at repatriation and compensation to the total exclusion of resettlement" (Joffe). This resolution clearly suggested that Palestinian refugees "should be allowed to return to their country of origin;" however, this resolution also extended to Jewish refugees and did not limit the options to only repatriation (Bartal). Payment for damages and resettlement were also possible solutions (Bartal). At the time of this resolution, the accepted solution for refugees was "resettlement in a third country" (El-Abed 535). This method for solving refugee crisis' can be seen in the millions of Germans, Indians, Pakistanis, Armenians, Greeks, Turks and other people groups who were "driven from their lands and resettled elsewhere" in the twentieth century (Nachmias). This resolution and these examples are evidence that in theory the return of refugees to their country of origin is the ideal of international law, but the real-life application of such laws has historically been of resettling refugees. Also, the assertion that Israelis' have "no responsibility whatsoever toward the descendants of the 1948 Palestinian refugees and no obligation to aid them other than out of purely humanitarian concerns" (Bartal) based on the population exchange that occurred between Israel and Arab states weakens the Palestinian claim to a right of return. This evidence should lead to the evaluation of resettlement as a valid and acceptable option at least equal to the right of return in legality.

Since 1948, many world leaders and average citizens have debated what to do about the Palestinian refugees, but this problem is not solvable by words alone. Actions are necessary. A timely solution would relieve Palestinian refugees of many of the woes and abuses that come from being a stateless people and eliminate growing obstacles to a solution before they become insurmountable. World leaders need to base this solution on the acceptance of Israel's Jewish-state and Arab nations' responsibility for the Palestinians in their countries. If these positions are accepted, resettlement should be the clear solution; furthermore, resettlement is realistic and has legal and historical backing. This controversial situation affects real people and will continue to have negative consequences until world leaders rise to the challenge and resettle and integrate the Palestinians.

Works Cited

Bartal, Shaul. "The Palestinian Refugee Problem Resolved." *Middle East Quarterly* 20.4 (2013): 29-40. Sociological Collection. Web. 5 Mar. 2014.

El-Abed, Oroub. "The Palestinians in Egypt: Identity, Basic Rights and Host State Policies." *Refugee Survey Quarterly* 28.2/3 (2009): 531-549. Political Science Complete. Web. 13 Mar. 2014.

Holzer, Elizabeth. "What Happens To Law in a Refugee Camp?." *Law & Society Review* 47.4 (2013): 837-872. SocINDEX with Full Text. Web. 9 Feb. 2014.

Ibrahim, Jennifer. "The Discrimination against Palestinian Refugees Living In Lebanon." *Palestine-Israel Journal of Politics, Economics & Culture* 15.1/2 (2008): 83-90. Business Source Complete. Web. 9 Feb. 2014.

Joffe, Alex. "UNRWA Resists Resettlement." *Middle East Quarterly*
19.4 (2012): 11-25. Political Science Complete. Web. 5
Mar. 2014.

Karsh, Efraim. "The War Against the Jews." *Israel Affairs* 18.3
(2012): 319. MasterFILE Premier. Web. 13 Mar. 2014.

Leckie, Scott, ed. *Housing, Land, and Property Restitution Rights
Of Refugees and Displaced Persons: Laws, Cases, and
Materials.* New York: Cambridge University Press, 2007. Print.

Marx, Emanuel. "Some UNRWA Refugees Have Resettled." *Middle
East Quarterly* 19.4 (2012): 37-44. Sociological Collection.
Web. 13 Mar. 2014.

Nachmias, Nitza. "UNRWA Betrays Its Mission." *Middle East
Quarterly* 19.4 (2012): 27-35. Political Science Complete.
Web. 5 Mar. 2014.

Peteet, Julie Marie. *Landscape of Hope and Despair: Palestinian
Refugee Camps.* n.p.: Philadelphia, Pa.: University of
Pennsylvania Press, 2005. Print.

Romirowsky, Asaf. "Washington's Failure to Rein In UNRWA."
Middle East Quarterly 19.4 (2012): 53-60. Political Science
Complete. Web. 5 Mar. 2014.

Weaver, Alain Epp. "Right of Return: Can the Palestinians Go
Home?." *Christian Century* 118.14 (2001): 8-9.
ATLASerials, Religion Collection. Web. 13 Mar. 2014.

"Confidence in the Classroom"
by Theresa Guillory

Instructor's Notes

In this paper, Theresa asks the question, "How can greater confidence be instilled in the writing classroom?". What research methods did she employ to answer this question? How is her essay organized? Are you convinced her proposed solution(s) would be effective? Why or why not?

Writers' Biography

Theresa Guillory is a sophomore Nursing major from Maryland. She discovered her love for writing during the 8th grade and has written several brief devotionals, poems, and essays in her spare time. Outside of her studies, Theresa enjoys running outdoors, reading novels, cooking, and spending time with her two sisters.

Confidence in the Classroom

Audible groans filled the classroom as the professor introduced the requirements of the first writing assignment. "Each of you will compose a six-page, double-spaced essay that is due in two weeks, discussing your opinion of one of Sigmund Freud's theories and providing a credible and persuasive argument supporting or opposing his ideas. In your composition, you must cite at least seven sources and follow MLA format, including a works cited page..." The instructor's voice continued, but each of the thirty students in the Freshman Composition class ignored the remainder of her words and focused instead on how they would survive the impending two weeks of torture. While one part of the class began to plan trips to the library for research, another portion of the group considered creative procrastination techniques to evade the agony of writing such an essay.

Freshman student Sarah Lewis, however, sat among her bewildered peers, attempting to conceal her tearfulness and contemplating how she belonged in the writing class under the tutelage of her Ph.D. level composition professor. Sarah had never been a strong writer and had no interest in Freud or argumentative essays. She felt out of place and isolated on her first day of class. Meanwhile, the professor continued to instruct her pupils, confident that the students would complete the course with a feeling of belonging among professional writers, unaware of Sarah's dilemma.

Sarah's predicament represents a dire problem confronting freshmen college students today. From the first moment that some freshmen students arrive in their writing classes and meet their accomplished professors, they hold the assumption that the instructors are a part of a lofty field and that they as inexperienced writers are outsiders. The freshmen's' single desire is to learn a few helpful tips to improve their skills. They don't aspire to anything higher, such as becoming a part of the writing field as accomplished composers. In her research study "A Stranger in Strange Lands: A College Student Writing across the Curriculum," Lucille Parkinson McCarthy observes that Dave, a freshman subject of the experiment, approaches each of his writing classes with different attitudes and expectations. In his Poetry class, a course with which he is the most unfamiliar, Dave views the class from the perspective of a stranger, attempting to grasp the subject, but failing to achieve the level of poetry interpretation and composition that he desires. His final grade of a C plus reflects his incomplete comprehension of the topics in the class. In her review of the results, McCarthy states that a large part of Dave's problem rests in the fact that though this student strives to perform at a maximum level in the class, he views himself as an outsider to the material that the professor presents. This attitude affects both his social interaction with his teacher and his other activity in the course (237-250). Many freshmen students identify with Dave in their feelings of incompetence and isolation within the writing field, as their attitudes influence their performance in the course and the grades they receive.

In addition to relating to Dave's experiences, some freshman students also connect with the pupils that Gary R. Hafer describes in "Ideas in Practice: Supplemental Instruction in Freshman Composition." Hafer comments that many students entering freshman composition courses not only dread but also despise the course. This may be due to their insufficient preparation for the college level writing field in previous years of education (par. 7). Inadequate preparation for the writing field in lower levels of education leads to freshmen's feelings of incompetence and isolation from the field of composition when they enter college writing courses.

These feelings of incompetence and isolation that freshmen writing students harbor are a grievous problem for college professors, for the students' views of the various writing arenas affect their grades and therefore reflect the professor's success or shortcomings in guiding the writing techniques of the students. Also, if college teachers don't accommodate students who feel incompetent and isolated from the field of writing, their pupils may develop negative views of them and spread their complaints, leading to unpleasant evaluations of the professors by their employers and fellow faculty members. As Hafer explains, unsuccessful instruction in composition courses may be an important cause of students' departure from college settings (par. 15). This endangers many aspects of a university, including attendance, funding and reputation. Students' departure from colleges due to ineffective writing classes therefore results in damage to both the professors' respectability and employment. Rick Evans, author of "Learning 'Schooled Literacy': The Literate Life Histories of Mainstream Student Readers and Writers," describes the disinterest in writing that many students develop in their adolescent years. These feelings of apathy may increase to the extent that students resent all writing tasks related to the academic field (319-339). Evans' observations reveal the gravity of the problem, as students' aversion to writing may emerge from thoughts of insecurity and inadequacy within the field of composition. The grave problem of some freshmen college students' low levels of performance in writing classes due to feelings of incompetence and isolation is one that college professors have the duty and ability to correct in an effective manner.

In correcting the issue of their freshmen student's feelings of incompetence and isolation within the writing field, college professors should avoid ineffective resolution strategies. One futile technique concerns separating the student who feels incompetent and isolated from his or her classmates and giving the pupil exclusive attention and assistance in developing proper writing skills. Though the professor may use this method in hopes of giving the student an added measure of comfort within the writing field, he will instead elevate the student's feelings of incompetence in writing and isolation from his or her peers. For instance, from the scenario in the beginning of the essay, if Sarah Lewis's professor recognized her anxiety in the class and brought attention to her predicament in the presence of her classmates, the resulting humiliation would reinforce Sarah's attitudes of displacement in the composition course.

In addition to the ineffective solution of drawing harmful attention to the individual student who feels incompetent and isolated, the possible resolution strategy of accommodating uncomfortable students by permitting them to write about anything they desire is also unsuccessful. Some freshmen students entering the college level writing arena feel uneasy and inadequate due to self-concepts of incompetence in the topics of their assignments. If the professors attempt to solve this predicament by forsaking the requirements for the assignment subject matter, however, the students may take advantage of this freedom and choose oversimplified topics, neglecting to strive for excellence within the writing field. In today's culture, adolescents display indifference in various areas including writing topics that do not relate to them. Margo Guillory, a homeschooling mother, attests that a lesser social pressure on students to apply themselves in settings that are irrelevant to them exists. This leads to attitudes of entitlement among students to only write about topics that amuse or connect to them in some way (Personal interview). Thus, this strategy of allowing students to write about anything they desire doesn't resolve the situation, but instead reinforces students' attitudes of entitlement. This solution also hampers the students' academic performance, a result that opposes the teachers' initial goals for their students in writing classes.

Because of the harmful effects and insufficient results of these two possible solutions, professors should abstain from using them. Although some individuals might disagree with its effectiveness, an alternative approach is possible that involves the teachers' acts of diminishing feelings of incompetence and isolation among freshmen students in the field of composition by allowing students to view themselves as a part of the writing profession and connecting the topics of writing assignments to the students. This approach includes the use of in-class peer review workshops, professor-student revision meetings, and a limited range of assignment subjects. Its effectiveness and practicality makes this strategy the best method for resolving low levels of performance due to attitudes of incompetence and isolation.

The use of in-class peer review workshops aids the effectiveness of the approach involving the incorporation of freshmen students as competent writers within the field of composition. When freshmen students receive the opportunity to review the writing of their peers and suggest changes, attitudes of confidence and proficiency in writing replace feelings of incompetence or isolation, as students attain an active role in the writing field. Furthermore, self-images of alienation from the writing field disappear as students operate as professionals, editing and discussing others' compositions. As a freshman in Dr. Wood's Composition course at Cedarville University, I had similar feelings of incompetence within the writing arena at the beginning of the course. Through in-class peer review sessions, however, I began to view myself as a capable individual in the writing field as I read the compositions of my classmates and proposed plausible revision strategies. A practical way to incorporate this method into teaching is by planning at least one workshop per writing assignment in the course of the semester so that students have the opportunity to edit one another's papers, yet there is a sufficient amount of additional class periods to hold lectures and perform other activities. This technique of in-class peer review workshops is a practical and effective way for professors to integrate freshmen students who feel inadequate within the writing field, along with the second component of the effective solution that encompasses professors providing opportunities for individualized conferences with their students.

The professors' use of conferences with their students in an exclusive setting adds to the success of the resolution strategy of integrating freshmen students into the writing field. As McCarthy's concludes from her experiment, part of Dave's difficulties in his poetry class result from his insufficient correspondence with his professor (256). If Dave's poetry professor had held conferences with each of his students to discuss their compositions, Dave would have felt more confident in his abilities and thus would have had a greater potential to achieve higher grades and mastery of the course. Furthermore, conferences between a professor and a student allow the teachers to explain the expectations for each writing assignment and permit students to ask questions regarding their papers on a level that is not possible in a classroom setting. Often, freshmen students feel incompetent and isolated from the field of writing within their composition classes because they don't grasp all the requirements or facets of their assignments. Conferences with the student's writing professors help to resolve this issue by clarifying any vague components of the professor's expectations for the student's paper. Individualized conferences are also practical for professors because sessions can have a limited time allotment, thus requiring a minimal number of hours outside of the classroom. Furthermore, conferences with students demonstrate the genuine care that the professors have for their pupils, earning the esteem of adolescents, faculty members, and supervisors. This component of the solution to accommodate isolated students within the writing field serves the same purpose as the final part of the resolution strategy that involves a limited range of assignment topics.

The last portion of this successful method involves professors allowing students to choose from a limited range of assignment topics. Sarah Lewis's professor designated a specific topic for her argumentative essay, making her feel intimidated on the first day of class and cultivating her feelings of incompetence and isolation. While those who oppose this approach may prefer to choose the faulty method by allowing students to choose whichever topics they desire, the effective strategy allows teachers to select a predetermined list of relevant yet challenging topics from which the writing students can select. This technique diminishes students' feelings of entitlement and promotes self-concepts as competent writers, for students who feel inadequate in the writing field can choose a topic from the list that they feel qualified to address in their compositions. They are also able to refine their writing skills by constructing their papers to meet the expectations and goals of their professors. College writing instructors should make the assignment subject matter in their writing classes more relevant to the way students think without compromising the original academic standards of the teachers (Guillory, Personal interview). Professors can accomplish this in a practical way by first asking for their student's input as to what topics interest them such as current events that concern young adults, or history topics that motivate the writing students. They should then permit the pupils to select a topic from the list throughout the semester. Professors may even choose a variant of this method, using a wide and pre-selected list of topics that relate to students and give them confidence at the beginning of the course, then narrowing the options and introducing new and unfamiliar assignment subjects over the course of the semester to further challenge the students and alert them of their ability to write about foreign topics with the same level of mastery in composition as with well-known subjects. Allowing students to compose papers on topics that relate to them helps to decrease freshmen student's feelings of incompetence and isolation, yet challenges the pupils to strive for excellence within the writing field.

Sarah Lewis' feelings of incompetence and isolation no longer existed as she sat in her usual place in the Freshman Composition class with the desire to pursue excellence in her writing. Over the course of the semester, Sarah's professor had guided the students through in-class peer review sessions, provided opportunities for individualized conferences with the students, and broadened the list of assignment topics to include matters that related to Sarah and her peers in the class. Sarah had lost her self-appraisal of an outsider to the field of composition. She viewed herself a member of the writing profession and would approach each of her academic writing tasks with feelings of confidence.

Works Cited

Evans, Rick. "Learning 'Schooled Literacy': The Literate Life Histories of Mainstream Student Readers and Writers." *Discourse Processes* 16.3 (1993): 317-340. *Class Moodle.* Web. 28 Nov. 2013.

Guillory, Margo. Personal interview. 4 Dec. 2013.

Hafer, Gary R. "Ideas in Practice: Supplemental Instruction in Freshman Composition." *Journal of Developmental Education* 24.3 (2001): pars. 1-41. *Academic Search Complete.* Web. 9 Nov. 2013.

McCarthy, Lucille P. "A Stranger in Strange Lands: A College Student Writing Across the Curriculum." *Research in the Teaching of English* 21.3 (1987): 233-265. *JSTOR.* Web. 27 Nov. 2013.

"Why Don't We Write?"
by Jeremiah Beatham

Instructor's Notes

"Why Don't We Write?" is an example of a Problem-Solution essay. At the end of the required semester of composition, the instructor asked Jeremiah and his classmates to identify problems in composition theory and pedagogy. Students were able to participate in the ongoing academic discourses about composition and composition theories in order to write papers that were academically relevant to the field of composition studies. In the first part of the paper, Jeremiah identifies a serious problem that besets many composition students—the lack of motivation students have in composition classes. Jeremiah identifies who can solve the problem and then uses deductive arguments to explain how the solution he suggests will solve the student-problem of lack of motivation in a composition course. Examine how Jeremiah integrates scholarly articles about composition theory and his own voice to identify the problem and then to move beyond complaining in order to solve the problem.

Writers' Biography

Jeremiah Beatham is a second-year Industrial Design major from Mexico-- just a regular guy who isn't used to writing things that stick out to people. He's just as shocked as you are that he's in this book, because typically he likes to make things with this hands or spend time outside, hopefully with good friends and family.

Why Don't We Write?

Scritch, scratch, scuff, scuff. The sounds are of a pencil laying down graphite as fast as the young man can think until he pauses, erases, re-writes, brushes the rubber wisps off the page, and reads over his work. He sets his mechanical pencil down on the bed next to him, leans against the poster-collage of a wall, and sorts through the lines in the Moleskine, reciting his poem out loud, composed in the excitement and thrill of a girl he's been dating. She's something special, so he's been writing all evening, trying to capture his feelings for her. He's motivated, to say the least. Another writer stations himself on the opposite side of the room, typing away at his cold, gray desk. Clackety-clack, tap-tap-tap. The sounds of this composition are much slower, and the author does not take time in poring over his work, trying to capture the slightest detail. Rather, this student stays up late because he has put off his writing assignment until the day before it was due. Why? Because he is not motivated. In fact, he's neglected this assignment for weeks, and knows that once he turns the paper in, all he is going to get is purple pen marks for his labor. Not red lip marks like his fellow writer.

The biggest problem with Composition classes is the lack of motivation for students. The problem starts when students are given assignments that don't relate directly to them. The tedious writing practice may call to an English major, or a writing-intensive major, but to the average student, there is nothing exciting in writing an essay, about something that does not interest them. As Lucille Parkinson McCarthy summarized, in her article "A Stranger in Strange Lands: A College Student Writing Across the Curriculum," students write best on topics that they find relevant and exciting (245). A problem is created because the papers that student write do not relate to them, meaning students do not have any motivation to learn more about the topic that they are discussing.

The problem of motivation augments with the grading process. Students formulate paragraph after paragraph, only to hand it to the teacher, who then straps the piece to his Procrustean table to be hacked down to size. No student wants to turn in an essay that they know is going to be graded and handed back with no real application. Not only do student write papers that are graded and archived, but they are forced to write paper after paper, each one only standing for hours of work that will be covered in purple and then hidden forever. Students are not motivated to write for the sake of writing, but for the sake of producing something that the teacher wants. In the case of Dave Garrison, each work that he produced was simply what he thought the teacher wanted, and dedicated only as much time to each paper as he thought the teacher would like (McCarthy 244). Students realize that they are simply carrying out the task of producing paper after paper, and are not motivated to invest in each one.

Writing teachers have the key to solving this problem. Because the problem of motivation dictates how much a student works on their paper, fixing this problem will reflect well on the teacher's effectiveness, as well as the student's grades. Teachers can do many things to motivate students—if teachers help students find a topic that they are interested in, allow and mandate that students revise their papers repeatedly, and finally, if teachers give papers a purpose, then students will be motivated.

The first step, choosing a relatable topic, is perhaps the easiest to accomplish. While some students in creative writing classes may be able to choose a subject, a writing class usually confines the students to a single idea, and forces each student to write on the same topic. This election means that whether or not the student is interested in igneous rocks, they must write about them. The solution for this is to give the students the task of writing about their own majors, hobbies, or something that means a lot to them. In an article "Learning 'Schooled Literacy': The Literate Life Histories of Mainstream Student Readers and Writers," Rick Evans summarizes the story of how one particular student, Kelly, began her writing career with a craft, in which she made a plate for her parents, as a gift (320). Her affection for her parents motivated her to make the plate, and do the writing. Evans goes on to explain how Kelly was later forced to do writing, when she was forced to write letters to her grandmother (302). The writing was not motivated, because the girl did not want to write to her grandmother. Teachers must allow students to write on whatever topic interests them most—probably something in their major, or their favorite classes or activities. The focus on something that interests the student will motivate them to write about it.

Some may suggest that the best way to allow people to write freely would be to teach a creative-writing style. This approach misses the importance of being relevant, however, as the creativity in writing classes does not actually allow for a variety of topic, but requires students to write in a poetic, story-like format. This format, while being easy to read and write, does not have many applications that are relevant to students. In my own life, having taken two creative writing classes, I gained nothing from these classes for writing—they were merely an outlet to express my creativity. The writing I did in that class was not revised, outside of minor grammar and spelling, because it was raw creativity—exactly what the teacher wanted. The stories and poems, once written, found their way into my mother's stash of memorabilia from my childhood, and have yet to be read again. Having creative writing classes would not allow for students to be motivated then, because they only express a very narrow part of their lives, and with no final motivation.

The second part of the solution that teachers can implement is restricting the work to one paper. While this sounds rather foolish and rash, the outcome would be much better-processed papers. In her article "Revision Strategies of Student Writers and Experienced Adult Writers," Nancy Sommers discusses the differences between writers in schools and those who have practiced writing for a long time. Those who had practiced revised their essays much more, deleting and re-arranging pages and paragraphs, in contrast to the student writers who would revise sentences or words (382-385). The comparison makes the distinction that the experienced writers are motivated to revise their work more because they have rethought it from different angles, given the paper time, and have established their thoughts on the topic. The advantage of having one paper for the composition course would be that students could continually revise their single essay all semester. Having one topic, one essay, and several deadlines to turn in revisions, all while being taught how to revise thoroughly would allow students to write to the best of their ability, dedicating time to one paper, and motivating them to have a nearly "perfect" essay in the end. The motivation would allow the student to understand the ideas that they have, as well as further their interests in the topic of choice.

Some teachers take the opposite approach to writing courses, requiring students to write several papers to get the maximum practice possible. This approach while pressuring students to put out many papers, ultimately would not work in motivating the students, as the students would not spend much time with each paper, only revising slightly before they were forced to turn in the next paper. The large load would also seem insurmountable, and would discourage students from writing, rather than motivating them to try to perfect their work.

Finally, the third part of the solution would be the purpose of the paper. I will define the purpose as who will see the paper, and what will be done with the paper after the student has written and edited it. Teachers read many papers each year, but none of these papers make it beyond the audience of the teacher. For instance, a teacher will grade this paper and hand it back to the author, who will then stuff it in his homework folder. No one sees the paper beyond the teacher, student, and perhaps a writing mentor. If the paper were not only graded, but also published for other students and experts in the area of the topic to read, students would be motivated. Dave Garrison wrote several papers, tailoring each one to the specific desires of the teacher he was writing for. The difference in teachers determined his writing style, and motivated how and what he wrote. He only said what he thought the teacher wanted to hear (McCarthy 243). Students should have their essays graded, then published before an audience of peers and those interested in the subject being discussed, because it would allow the students to write more openly and thoroughly about their topic, being motivated with the goal of contributing to an audience and an academic discussion. Garrison continues to explain how writing is a community-motivated idea and a social function (234-235). Publishing papers would allow students to express their ideas and research from their perspective to a group that can understand and relate to the topic. The community motivates students, as they are contributing with their writing, not monologue-ing for a teacher.

Scritch, clackety-scratch, scuff-tap, scuff-click tap tap. The sounds are of a pair of writers, on both sides of the room, writing furiously as they compose a work, poem or paper, which they feel expresses themselves and relates to them. A piece that they have put time and effort into, and know will mean something once they are done writing. And while both may not get red lip marks for their work, neither will incur the dreaded purple pen marks.

Works Cited

Evans, Rick. "Learning "Schooled Literacy": The Literate Life Histories of Mainstream Student Readers and Writers." *Discourse Processes* 16 (1993) : Moodle Class Page. Web. 5 Dec. 2013.

McCarthy, Lucille Parkinson. "A Stranger in Strange Lands: A College Student Writing Across the Curriculum." *Research in the Teaching of English* 21.3 (1987) : JSTOR. Web. 5 Dec. 2013.

Sommers, Nancy. *Revision Strategies of Student Writers and Experienced Adult Writers.* Washington D.C.: National Institute of Education, 1982. Web.

"The Solution to Dangerous Antibiotic-resistant Bacteria" by Ryan Marquardt

Instructor's Notes

The technical nature of Ryan Marquardt's research paper could make it difficult for the average reader to understand, but Ryan not only makes his points clear and easily accessible to a general audience, but he also makes them interesting. How is he able to able to accomplish clarity? Accessibility? And interest? Is there any point in the essay where you find yourself wishing to know more?

Writers' Biography

Ryan Marquardt is a junior Molecular and Cellular Biology major from Michigan. Ryan enjoys learning and discovering new things in the realm of biology and writing about them. His hobbies include reading the classics and essays on philosophy and religion, as well as playing guitar and working outdoors.

The Solution to Dangerous Antibiotic-resistant Bacteria

Infectious diseases have ravaged the human race unchecked in various places and times for millennia. When people think of widespread diseases and infections that have historically plagued humanity, often their minds go to the Middle Ages, a time when sanitation and living conditions had not caught up with the mass urbanization of Western society. Bacterial sicknesses like Bubonic Plague became major crises that killed multitudes of people in certain areas. In fact, Bubonic Plague killed as many as 40 million people (Bugl). Finally, during the 1940s when antibiotics such as penicillin became widely available, infectious disease death rates declined dramatically, and such diseases have since caused no significant trouble for the developed world (Interagency Task Force on Antimicrobial Resistance 3). However, microbial diseases are not simply a danger of the past; some infections, even in modern America, have antibiotic resistant strains. These strains hold the potential for devastating populations by overcoming modern medicine. In the words of one source, "Multidrug-resistance organisms are one of the world's top health problems" (Lilley et al 608). Currently, several types of Staph, Strep, Tuberculosis, Salmonella, E. coli, and many other infectious diseases strongly resist antibiotic treatment (CDC Office of Infectious Diseases 16-17). Antibiotic resistant bacteria present a major medical problem for modern humanity, and although many different solutions have potential, medical professionals must control bacterial resistance by cooperating with patients on a combination of strict hospital protocol and limited use of antibiotic medication.

While bacterial illness is a major problem that the medical world must address, bacteria do not cause every type of disease. A prerequisite for the study of antibiotic resistance is to know that humans also face the problem of viruses. The key difference between a bacterium and a virus is that a bacterium is a complete cell, capable of living on its own, whereas a virus must infect an already living cell. Antibiotics can only kill bacteria, not viruses, because they interfere in different ways with the life process of the bacterium cell as a whole. If researchers and doctors used this same strategy against viruses, they would kill normal body cells along with the viruses. Therefore, the issue of antibiotic resistance applies only to bacterial diseases.

Obviously, bacteria are the cause of bacterial diseases. In her article "Antibiotics and the Rise of Superbugs," Georgina Casey, director of Continuing Professional Development for Nurses, explains that "bacteria are prokaryotes, which are single-cell organisms lacking a nucleus or other membrane-bound organelles," and they can be harmful if they directly attack cells or produce toxins that damage cell processes (20). Although various types of harmful bacteria are everywhere, under normal circumstances epithelial tissue barriers such as skin and the walls of the digestive tract work with the immune system to keep these dangerous microbes in check. When the bacteria are able to reproduce quickly and overwhelm the immune system, however, the human body has problems. Like a swarm of locusts on desert vegetation, bacteria can quickly shut down the processes necessary to sustain life, kill the individual, and go on to reproduce and infect the next person. That is how deadly epidemics such as Bubonic Plague killed so many in the past.

The advent of antibiotic medication in the mid Twentieth

Century staggeringly improved human control over bacterial infection. Since bacteria differ from human body cells in structure and function, "antimicrobial drugs have been developed that can damage or kill the prokaryotic cell with minimal harm to the human host" (Casey 20). In essence, the drug impairs the bacteria's ability to reproduce and spread. Depending on the specific case, an antibiotic will remove bacteria's ability to either make its own food, synthesize structural elements, uncoil DNA for replication, or sustain life in other ways. Regardless of the mechanism, the ultimate purpose of an antibiotic is to reduce the bacteria population in the person enough that the body's immune system can cope with the invasion (Casey 22). Without antibiotics, modern day surgical operations and other treatments would simply be unrealistic because of the risk of bacterial infection, according to Arias and Murray, both professors of medicine at Texas Medical School of Houston (439). Little would be the same in medicine without antibiotics.

Unfortunately, antibiotic medication is no longer a "magic pill" that holds the answer to all cases of bacterial infection. Because of their rapid rates of reproduction, bacteria commonly develop genetic mutations in their DNA, and these changes can occasionally cause a benefit to the microbe in its defense against antibiotics (Casey 23). Before the invention of antibiotics, this would not have mattered because the non-mutated bacterium reproduced uncontrollably anyway. However, once antibiotics came into common usage, these mutated bacteria began to outlive the original type and continue reproduction. Over time, the mutated strain would make up the majority of the population, and the antibiotic that had previously been effective would no longer help. Since multiple types of antibiotics can be useful, this may not cause a dangerous situation in the short term. Simply administering a different antibiotic that the bacteria had no resistance to would succeed in controlling it, though perhaps not as effectively. The real problem is that bacteria constantly mutate, and the strain that survives and reproduces more will become the dominant group. This means that if a bacterium mutates again and obtains some sort of mechanism to resist the new drug, the new strain will survive exposure to both antibiotics. Over time, a species of bacteria may build resistance to all relevant antibiotics in this manner and leave an infected patient untreatable.

Although this phenomenon of resistance sounds dangerous

on a scientific level, the practical peril is even more frightening. The CDC Office of Infectious Diseases (OID) reports that each year between bacterial and fungal infections that have a resistance to the antibiotic designed to treat them, over 20 million illnesses and 23,000 deaths occur (13). For a culture that tends to believe modern medicine has infections and bacterial diseases completely under control, that is a devastating amount of illness and death. Humans can pick up microbes in many different ways such as E. coli in tainted water or meat or MRSA entering through the open wound of a surgical site in a hospital. Because of the incredible variety in bacteria, finding a single solution is completely unrealistic, and this makes fixing the problem even harder. Even if medicine brings one microbe under control, one that harms in a different way or spreads differently may spring up in its place. The practical danger is obvious.

Antibiotic resistant bacteria present such a real problem because of their unpredictable ability to change, making appropriate antibiotics useless. Theoretically, any harmful bacteria could develop dangerous resistance to several drugs and become an epidemic. Since this is such a relevant threat, many microbiologists and medical professionals are exploring different options to defeat microbes. Some would say that researchers must simply continue to stay ahead of bacteria by formulating new antibiotics to treat a disease before the old ones become ineffective. Arias and Murray explain that "a concerted effort on the part of academic researchers and their institutions, industry, and government is crucial" to formulate new antibiotics that can successfully exterminate resistant bacteria before they become resistant to all currently available antibiotics (443). Ideally for humans, it would work out this way and a new antibiotic would simply wipe out a bacteria. However, since the original antibiotic did not exterminate the bacteria before it developed resistance, assuming that a new antibiotic would wipe it out is unrealistic, and it also presumes upon the fact that researchers will actually invent new antibiotics for all dangerous bacterial infections. While new research is important, and this solution is theoretically possible, humans cannot count on it in the short term to prevent a major outbreak of an antibiotic resistant disease that could kill many. In addition, society cannot view simply inventing new antibiotics to keep bacteria that have developed resistance to other medications in check as a long term solution because at some point researchers will run out of options in ways to kill bacteria with antibiotics. Other types of solutions are necessary now and most likely also necessary for long term control of bacteria.

One novel solution researchers are currently developing is the use of nanosilver to combat antibiotic resistant E. coli and other microbes (Dugal and Chakraborty 498). In this treatment, silver particles disrupt the respiration of the bacteria which cuts off their ability to use energy and kills them (Dugal and Chakraborty 498). The benefits of this treatment include the fact that "silver has a far lower propensity to induce microbial resistance than antibiotics," and "has been known to be nontoxic to humans in low concentrations" (Dugal and Chakraborty 498). Although this is a fairly new treatment, and more research is necessary before doctors can widely implement it, it has significant potential in the future. The problem right now is that no one fully knows all the potential side effects, and even if it works perfectly, it is expensive and only fights against E. coli and Pseudomonas, not other antibiotic resistant bacteria (Dugal and Chakraborty 500). Again, this solution is one that vulnerable humans cannot fully count on at this point to solve the problem of even one or two types of bacteria, let alone all types of bacteria.

A slightly more hopeful solution under current research is furthering the use of vaccinations rather than antibiotics. Dr. Charles Knirsch, a senior administrator for a major medical research company, said in an interview, "I think the future, though, will be individual manipulation of the immune system, not just as immune suppressives but as immune adjuvants...I do think that vaccines will be used on individual patients both preventively but also therapeutically." Although he admits he does not know the specifics of how this would work, Knirsch sees immune system manipulation as a hopeful future solution once someone develops it with further research. Solutions like this would dramatically impact the fight against antibiotic resistance, but again, an effective invention is not inevitable. Since this treatment is not currently available, standing by waiting for researchers to formulate it will not help the problem now.

Aiming at immediate solutions, Toby Butler, a Quality Improvement Specialist for the Oklahoma Foundation for Medical

Quality, presents a very practical, tangible strategy. He asserts that medical professionals should treat the multi-drug resistant (MDR) bacteria problem like a pest infestation by systematically seeking and destroying sources of the bacteria before they spread (13). Better hospital sanitation protocol and policies are his proposed solution, and he has good reason. Recent statistics show that "health care-associated infections develop in approximately 10% of hospitalized patients, and the cost of treating these infections amounts to $4 to $11 billion annually," and they are usually acquired from various medical instruments (Lilley et al 586). Lilley et al also goes on to report that at least 70% of hospital related infections are avoidable (586). Since so many antibiotic resistant infections spread in a hospital setting, eliminating bacteria's ability to transfer from patient to patient would choke off an infection's growth and solve a majority of the problem. While this approach does not help patients who have already contracted an infection, it does prevent future problems. If professionals perfectly execute this plan, it could even eliminate much of the need for antibiotics in the first place. This solution would require some practical research on how infections spread in the hospital in order to find out where the focus needs to be on preventing transfer of microbes. One example of this already happening is a study done by Usha, Kumar, and Gopal in which they discovered MDR bacteria in hospital sewage (45). This raises the need for better sterilization of sewage before it is released from the hospital. Besides creating new protocol, this preventative solution could also require more training for medical professionals and potentially necessitate more personnel to oversee implementation of stricter policies. All of these steps would cost money and possibly inconvenience hospital staff, but together they are a very practical and simple solution to limit the spread of any type of bacteria and reduce the need for antibiotics, which would ultimately save lives and money.

Another potential solution to resistant bacteria that is very practical and would save lives is to avoid overprescribing antibiotics and only use them when absolutely necessary. Ever since antibiotic medication became available, many doctors have gotten into the habit of playing it safe and prescribing antibiotics to any patient whose illness they thought might possibly be rooted in bacteria. Although this practice does help many patients recover more quickly, it greatly increases the amount of antibiotics in use and aids bacteria's ability to develop resistance. Physicians must act on the knowledge that the fewer antibiotics they utilize, the less the bacteria will develop resistance to the antibiotics for when they are absolutely needed (Thomas et al 2065). Similar to improving sanitation protocol, this takes discernment and discipline on the part of medical professionals. If doctors are willing to wait longer to prescribe antibiotics until they are sure they are necessary, it will cut down on antibiotic resistance. Unfortunately, this may cause more patient discomfort or even death since immediately treatable patients have to wait a few days to receive it until the doctor is sure they do, in fact, need the medication. On the other hand, this method is not expensive like many of the other proposed solutions but rather will save money, and it will help reduce the resistance of every type of infection which will ultimately save lives.

A similar simple, practical, and inexpensive solution is patient education. Patients who misuse their antibiotics by overusing them or taking them at the wrong times or improperly using them in other ways contribute to antibiotic resistance because they are essentially wasting them and causing more antibiotic use than necessary. The obvious drawbacks to this solution are that doctors cannot actually follow patients around everywhere to make sure they follow instructions, and the overall effect of even perfect use by patients will probably be fairly small. However, this is a solution that is easy and inexpensive to implement and could aid in the fight to limit antibiotic resistance.

In reality, the best solution to antibiotic resistance is a combination of several proposed solutions. While research is important, and new cures are very helpful, they are not inevitable. For now, focusing on the practical, controllable aspects of limiting antibiotic resistance is the most helpful. Hospital staff must put extra effort into proper hospital sanitation around the world even if it is difficult and inconvenient. The best way to snuff out a disease is to cut it off from spreading. Doctors also must be willing to make tough choices in administering antibiotics instead of just prescribing them in the hope that they help a patient. First, he or she must be certain antibiotics will eradicate the infection from the patient, and then he or she may prescribe them. In addition, medical professionals must put more effort into public awareness of the danger of antibiotic resistant bacteria. Proper education will give patients motivation to use antibiotics properly and assist in proper sanitation efforts. If doctors, nurses, pharmacists, and patients do all they can at the practical level in hospitals, antibiotics will stay useful when they are truly necessary, and MDR bacterial superbugs will not run rampant.

Although many in modern American society are ignorant to the modern danger of bacterial infection and disease, experts agree that it is a serious problem. Human health is fast approaching the edge of a cliff. As more bacterial infections mutate and become invincible to current antibiotics, modern medicine must answer the call and provide workable solutions for them. If humans do not want to experience another plague reminiscent of the Middle Ages, experts say something must change. While researchers continue their important search for new cures which may or may not exist, medical professionals and patients must understand the real danger of antibiotic resistance and work together to stop it by cutting off transmission in the hospital setting and by properly using the antibiotics that are currently available. A concerted effort on everyone's part, doctor, patient, and researcher alike, is necessary if humanity is to outlive pathogenic bacteria.

Works Cited

Arias, Cesar A, and Barbara E Murray. "Antibiotic-Resistant Bugs in the 21st Century--A Clinical Super-Challenge." *The New England Journal of Medicine* 360.5 (2009): 439-443. Web. 22 Sept. 2013.

Bugl, Paul. "History of Epidemics and Plagues." University of Hartford. Oct. 2001. Web. 1 Oct. 2013.

Butler, Toby. "Extermination: Utilizing Risk Management To Quash 'Super Bugs.'" *Oklahoma Nurse* 55.1 (2010): 13. Web. 22 Sept. 2013.

Casey, Georgina. "Antibiotics and the Rise Of Superbugs." *Kai Tiaki Nursing New Zealand* 18.10 (2012): 20-24. Web. 20 Sept. 2013.

CDC Office of Infectious Diseases (OID). "Antibiotic Resistance Threats in the United States 2013." Centers for Disease Control and Prevention. 2013. Web. 28 Sept. 2013.

Dugal, S., and S. Chakraborty. "Biogenic Synthesis of Nanosilver and its Antibacterial Effect Against Resistant Gram Negative

Pathogens." *International Journal Of Pharmacy & Pharmaceutical Sciences* 5.3 (2013): 498-501. Web. 19 Oct. 2013.

Interagency Task Force on Antimicrobial Resistance. "2011 Progress Towards Implementation of: A Public Health Action Plan to Combat Antimicrobial Resistance." Centers for Disease Control and Prevention. 2011. Web. 26 Sept. 2013.

Knirsch, Charles. "Dr. Charles Knirsch: 'These Are Not Ruthless Decisions'." Frontline. PBS, 22 Oct. 2013. Web. 30 Oct. 2013.

Lilley, Linda L., Shelly R. Collins, Scott Harrington, and Julie S. Snyder. *Pharmacology and the Nursing Process.* 6th ed. St. Lois: Mosby Elsevier, 2011. 586-608. Print.

Thomas, Reema et al. "Emergence Of 'Super Bug' And Use Of Antibiotics: What We Learned, What We Have Yet To Learn?." *Journal of Pharmacy Research* 4.7 (2011): 2064-2066. Web. 22 Sept. 2013.

Usha, K., E. Kumar, and Sai Gopal DVR. "Occurrence of Various Beta-Lactamase Producing Gram Negative Bacilli in the Hospital Effluent." *Asian Journal of Pharmaceutical & Clinical Research* (2013): 42-46. Web. 19 Oct. 2013.

Composition Student Learning Outcomes

By the end of first year composition, students will:

- apply knowledge of conventions through proper formating, documenting, and structuring of written text, controlling such surface features as syntax, grammar, punctuation and spelling.
- use technology to locate and evaluate information as well as produce one's own writing.
- complete each stage of the writing process toward producing a cohesive text.
- respond appropriately to various rhetorical situations.
- apply critical researching, reading, and writing skills in order to integrate their own ideas with those of others.
- display a biblical worldview through written or oral coursework.

Grading System

A – Recognizes excellent achievement. It is indicative of superior quality work and reveals a thorough mastery of the subject matter. The student receiving this grade should demonstrate enough interest to do some independent investigation beyond the actual course requirements.

B – Indicates work and achievement that are well above average. The student receiving this grade should be capable of doing advanced work in this field. The quality of the work should be considered better than that achieved by the average student.

C – Indicates average achievement and a satisfactory meeting of requirements.

D – Reveals inferior accomplishment and is generally unsatisfactory from the standpoint of course requirements.

F – Failing grade. It indicates very unsatisfactory work. No course credit is earned.

AU – Given when a course is audited. To receive this notation, the student must attend and participate in the course. No credit is earned.

Plagiarism: What It is
and How to Recognize and Avoid It

What is Plagiarism and Why is it Important?

In college courses, we are continually engaged with other people's ideas: we read them in texts, hear them in lecture, discuss them in class, and incorporate them into our own writing. As a result, it is very important that we give credit where it is due. Plagiarism is using others' ideas and words without clearly acknowledging the source of that information.

How Can Students Avoid Plagiarism?

To avoid plagiarism, you must give credit whenever you use
- another person's idea, opinion, or theory;
- any facts, statistics, graphs, drawings—any pieces of information—that are not common knowledge;
- quotations of another person's actual spoken or written words; or
- paraphrase of another person's spoken or written words.

These guidelines are taken from the <u>Code of Student Rights, Responsibilities, and Conduct.</u>

Writing Resources

Cedarville University Writing Center

Director: Professor Julie Moore
Tyler Digital Communication Center
Room 104
Cedarville University
Phone: 937-766-3245
Email: The Writing Center

Mission

The Cedarville University Writing Center exists to help writers at all levels of proficiency from all academic disciplines develop effective writing skills. This development takes place primarily through one-on-one peer consultations which are adapted to individual writers' needs. Such consultations will be competent and timely, will occur in a comfortable, non-threatening atmosphere, and will address all writing projects in any stage of the writing process, from brainstorming to revision. These consultations focus primarily on the writing at hand, but the long-term goal for every session is to help each tutee become a better writer overall. The center is neither a proofreading service nor a classroom - tutors do not edit or grade. Instead, the center blends service and communication, a blend which at its core is wholly Christian.

Centennial Library

Department Contact Numbers

- Administration: 937-766-7845
- Circulation Desk: 937-766-7840
- Collection Services: 937-766-7844
- Curriculum Materials Center: 937-766-7854
- MediaPLEX: 937-766-7852
- Reference Desk: 937-766-7850
- Office FAX: 937-766-2337
- Public FAX: 937-766-3776

Hours

- Monday - Thursday: 7:45 am - 11:30 pm
- Friday: 7:45 am - 7:00 pm
- Saturday: 10:00 am - 7:00 pm
- Sunday: 7:30 pm - 11:30 pm